The Microsoft Outlook Ideas Book

Barbara March

PUBLISHING

BIRMINGHAM - MUMBAI

The Microsoft Outlook Ideas Book

Copyright © 2006 Packt Publishing

All rights reserved. No part of this book may be reproduced, stored in a retrieval system, or transmitted in any form or by any means, without the prior written permission of the publisher, except in the case of brief quotations embedded in critical articles or reviews.

Every effort has been made in the preparation of this book to ensure the accuracy of the information presented. However, the information contained in this book is sold without warranty, either express or implied. Neither the author, Packt Publishing, nor its dealers or distributors will be held liable for any damages caused or alleged to be caused directly or indirectly by this book.

Packt Publishing has endeavored to provide trademark information about all the companies and products mentioned in this book by the appropriate use of capitals. However, Packt Publishing cannot guarantee the accuracy of this information.

First published: February 2006

Production Reference: 1150206

Published by Packt Publishing Ltd.
32 Lincoln Road
Olton
Birmingham, B27 6PA, UK.

ISBN 1-904811-70-1

www.packtpub.com

Cover Design by www.visionwt.com

Credits

Author
Barbara March

Reviewers
Eric Woodford
Stuart Whyte
Catherine Fenner
Shawn K. Hall
Charles G. "Chuck" Boulais
"Dr. Frank" Kendralla Jr.

Technical Editor
Jimmy Karumalil

Editorial Manager
Dipali Chittar

Development Editor
Douglas Paterson

Indexer
Ashutosh Pande

Proofreader
Chris Smith

Production Coordinator
Manjiri Nadkarni

Cover Designer
Helen Wood

About the Author

Barbara March's long career in office administration, in many different industries, and her passion for computer software led her into software training. After obtaining Microsoft Office Specialist qualifications at Expert level and becoming a Microsoft MOUS Master Instructor, Barbara extended her knowledge and expertise further in MS Office by achieving outstanding pass marks in ECDL Advanced examinations. This knowledge and expertise, she has applied in all her posts including her current role as a data analyst in a local authority.

Barbara's analytical mind forces her to question the accepted boundaries of the software she uses and to apply her flair and imagination to find ways to use the software capabilities to the limit and to the benefit of her performance and professionalism.

Table of Contents

Preface

For me, this book is the journal of an exciting voyage of discovery—and it all began with a request for some training in Microsoft Outlook.

Unlike most of the training sessions I had conducted previously, I knew the students very well—the work they did, the environment in which they worked, and the constraints that they worked under. They were not only my students but also my work colleagues. So, knowing that I could direct the instruction to address their specific needs, I began to look deeper into Outlook, hoping to find some useful solutions to the challenges that I knew that my colleagues faced every day.

I was already a proficient Outlook user, but the more research I did, the less I found that I knew and one of the biggest revelations for me was that Outlook could perform calculations! However, how these calculations and other capabilities could be used by ordinary users (i.e. not programmers) seemed not to be documented, anywhere—until now!

I have had a lot of fun putting together these solutions and this book had to be written; these powerful Outlook features should not remain the sole realm of the programmers; we can use them too!

What This Book Covers

Chapter 1 discusses the Outlook Calendar folder and demonstrates ways in which calendar items and folders can be manipulated and presented to provide a valuable and professional, timesaving management tool.

In *Chapter 2*, we customize the view of Contacts records to produce an efficient client-business directory and a detailed and comprehensive personnel database. We also take a huge leap of imagination and explore the use of the Contacts folder to store the details of and manage objects such as company vehicles and meeting rooms.

Chapter 3 looks at Tasks and how they can help us, not only manage the day-to-day jobs we have to do, but also monitor time and cost in service processes. Tasks are also linked to Contacts to provide personalized records.

Chapter 4 presents two rounded solutions that bring together techniques from the previous chapters and are where all the Outlook components integrate into an efficient machine that belies any belief that Outlook is simply an email client.

What You Need to Use This Book

This book is about Microsoft Outlook and not Outlook Express. There are differences in functionality between the versions of Outlook, and where this affects the examples these differences have been noted and alternative instructions included.

If the reader is familiar with functions in Microsoft Access and Excel, he/she will have no difficulty understanding the functions used in the examples and their syntax. For readers without this experience, the instructions are clear and easy to follow.

Conventions

In this book, you will find a number of styles of text that distinguish between different kinds of information. Here are some examples of these styles, and an explanation of their meaning.

There are three styles for code. Code words in text are shown as follows: "We can include other contexts through the use of the include directive."

A block of code will be set as follows:

```
Sub cmdPrint_Click()
    Set oWordApp = CreateObject("Word.Application")
    If oWordApp Is Nothing Then
        MsgBox "Couldn't start Word."
    Else
        Dim oWordApp
        Dim oWordDoc
```

New terms and **important words** are introduced in a bold-type font. Words that you see on the screen, in menus or dialog boxes for example, appear in our text like this: "clicking the Next button moves you to the next screen".

> Warnings or important notes appear in a box like this.

Reader Feedback

Feedback from our readers is always welcome. Let us know what you think about this book, what you liked or may have disliked. Reader feedback is important for us to develop titles that you really get the most out of.

To send us general feedback, simply drop an email to feedback@packtpub.com, making sure to mention the book title in the subject of your message.

If there is a book that you need and would like to see us publish, please send us a note in the SUGGEST A TITLE form on www.packtpub.com or email suggest@packtpub.com.

If there is a topic that you have expertise in and you are interested in either writing or contributing to a book, see our author guide on www.packtpub.com/authors.

Customer Support

Now that you are the proud owner of a Packt book, we have a number of things to help you to get the most from your purchase.

Downloading the Example Code for the Book

Visit http://www.packtpub.com/support, and select this book from the list of titles to download any example code or extra resources for this book. The files available for download will then be displayed.

> The downloadable files contain instructions on how to use them.

Errata

Although we have taken every care to ensure the accuracy of our contents, mistakes do happen. If you find a mistake in one of our books—maybe a mistake in text or code—we would be grateful if you would report this to us. By doing this you can save other readers from frustration, and help to improve subsequent versions of this book. If you find any errata, report them by visiting http://www.packtpub.com/support, selecting your book, clicking on the Submit Errata link, and entering the details of your errata. Once your errata have been verified, your submission will be accepted and the errata added to the list of existing errata. The existing errata can be viewed by selecting your title from http://www.packtpub.com/support.

Questions

You can contact us at questions@packtpub.com if you are having a problem with some aspect of the book, and we will do our best to address it.

1

The Calendar Folder

The **Outlook Calendar** folder can be overlooked as a valuable storage area and source of information relating to diary events. This chapter will introduce you to ways of viewing your calendar that will enable you to extract quickly, and in professional formats, data relating to meetings and events without the need to replicate the data or use any other application or program.

In this chapter we will look at the following examples:

- A Meetings Schedule
- A Record of Goods or Services
- A Staff Leave Calendar
- A Staff Leave Calendar—Daily View By Department
- A Staff Leave Calendar—Sick Leave View
- A Calendar View that Records Conference Costs
- A Calendar View that Records Your Expenses
- A To Do List for Calendar Items

A Meetings Schedule

In a busy calendar, there will be a variety of events, teleconferences, appointments, visits, internal and external meetings, and at times it would be useful to extract and/or print schedules of particular types of calendar entry, such as a schedule of various current and future internal meetings.

Such a schedule can be produced by creating a table type view of the calendar that filters on items assigned to the internal meeting category, with start dates on or after the current date and that groups items by Subject.

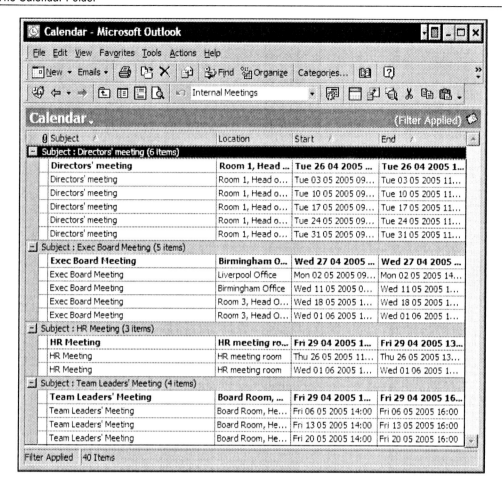

Creating the Calendar View

In the above example, all meetings within the organization have been assigned to the internal meeting category and the view highlights those meetings taking place within the current week. The steps to create the view above are as follows:

1. Create a category named internal meeting. To do this, first open the Categories dialog box by either right-clicking on any item in your calendar or selecting any item in your calendar and clicking the Categories option in the Edit menu. From the Categories dialog, click the Master Category List button, enter the name internal meeting in the New category: box, and click Add.

2. For those meetings in your calendar that are internal (in other words within your organization), assign them to the internal meeting category by right-clicking each item in the calendar, selecting Categories, and choosing the internal meeting category.

3. Create a new table type view from the Define Views | New option. In Outlook 2003 you will find this option under View | Arrange by | Current View | Define Views | New.

4. Name the view Internal Meetings.

5. In the View Summary dialog box (or View | Arrange by | Current View | Customize View in Outlook 2003), click Fields, and select the fields: Subject, Location, Start, and End, and click OK.

6. Set Group By to Subject.

7. Set Sort items by to Start.

8. From the Filter | More Choices | Categories option, select the internal meeting category we created above.

9. From the Filter | Advanced tab, create the following filter:

Field	Condition	Value
Start	on or after	today

10. From the Automatic Formatting option, click Add, and create the following formatting rule:

Formatting Rule Name	Field	Condition	Font Format
Current Week	Start	this week	Bold

Formatting Rule Name is known as Rules for this view: in Outlook 2003.

What Just Happened?

We have just created a simple but very useful view of a very busy calendar. The view has enabled us to simplify the calendar by extracting only certain items and condensing them into a neat table format that will enable us to plan and manage the items more easily.

The Result

The result, when printed, can produce a schedule to show either all or only selected meetings. The Internal Meetings heading of this report was created from the File menu | Print Preview | Page Setup | Header/Footer tab.

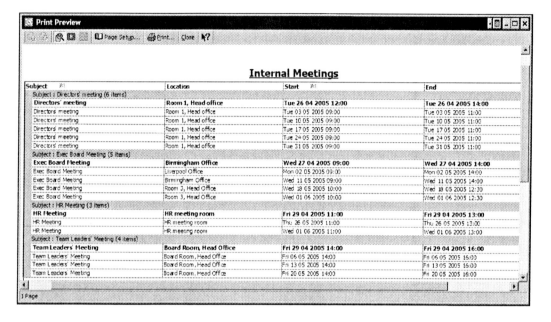

A Record of Goods or Services

A separate Outlook Calendar, reserved for the purpose, is also a convenient place to record the ordering or purchase of specific goods or services.

For example, if you are required to book taxis on a regular basis, make entries for these bookings in a calendar especially for taxi bookings. The Taxi Calendar in a Day/Week/Month type view may look something like this:

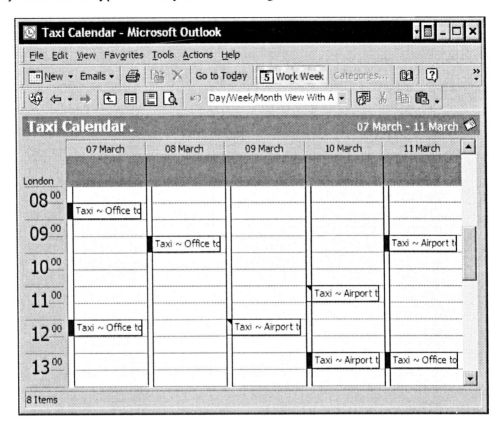

However, if we create a table type view of this calendar, as in the screen shot below, we can produce something that will allow us to analyze and print the data. This view will enable us to reconcile taxi company invoices and records and apportion the costs against the relevant members of staff.

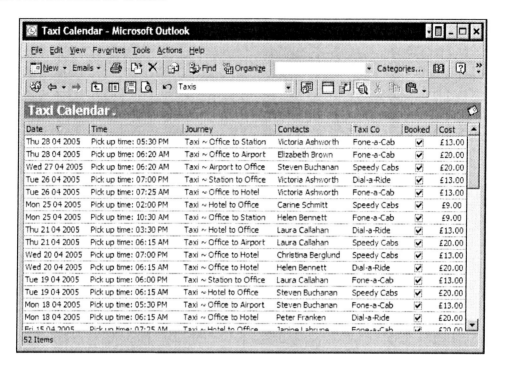

Creating the Calendar View

As this calendar contains only taxi bookings entries, the individual items need not be assigned to a category.

To create this view:

1. Create a new table-type view from the Define Views | New option and name the view Taxis.

2. In the View Summary dialog box (Customize view in Outlook 2003), click Fields, and select the fields: Subject, Start, and Contacts, and click OK.

3. We will now create the following three new manual fields using the New Field tab:

Name	Type	Format	Purpose
Taxi Co	Text	Text	To enter the name of the Taxi company.
Booked	Yes/No	Icon	To produce a check to indicate that the taxi booking has been made.
Cost	Currency	2 digits	To record the taxi fee obtained from the invoice.

4. We will also create the following Formula field:

Name	In the Formula Field window
Time	"Pick up time: " & Format([Start],"hh:mm AM/PM")

5. Exit the View Summary and from the Format Columns dialog box rename the following fields as follows:

Field name	New name	Format
Subject	Journey	
Start	Date	Choose a format that shows the day and date only.

What Just Happened?

We have constructed a view that will enable us to view the items in an organized and logical manner and that will make reconciling the taxi booking accounts much easier.

The only formula field in this view is the Time field and it performs two functions:

- Inserting the prefix text Pick up time: before the time
- Using the Format function to format the Start field to show the time only as hours and minutes adding AM or PM as appropriate

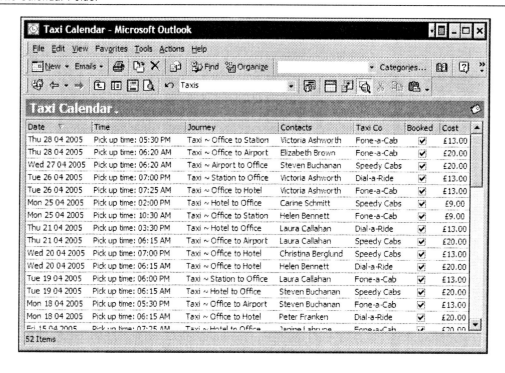

How to Use This View

1. Make the entry for the taxi booking in the calendar in the Day/Week/Month view.

2. Link the entry to the staff member concerned by clicking the Contacts button at the bottom left on the Appointments form and selecting the staff member from the Contacts folder.

3. When taxis have been booked, change to the Taxis view of the calendar, and click the icon in the Booked field.

4. When the invoices are received from the taxi companies, change to the Taxis view of the calendar to reconcile the bookings that are being invoiced and enter the charges in the Cost field.

The view can be manipulated to show the bookings in various ways.

*   **To view by a particular month**:

    From Customize Current View | Filter | Advanced tab add the following filter:

Field	Condition	Value
	this month	
	or	
Start	last month	
	or	
	between	first date and second date

- **To view by Taxi company**:

  Group on the Taxi Co field.

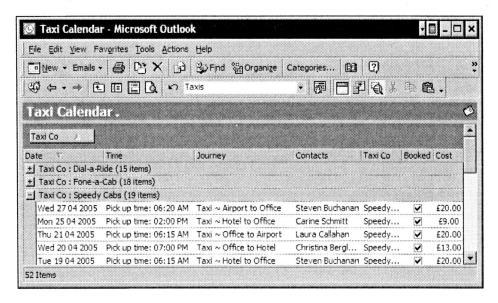

- **To view by staff member**:

  Group on the Contacts field.

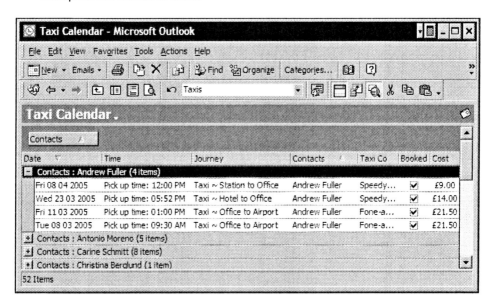

- **To view events on an individual Contact's record**:

  By linking the taxi bookings to the Contacts from the Contacts folder Properties | Activities tab, the taxi bookings will appear on the Activities tab of the individual Contact's record.

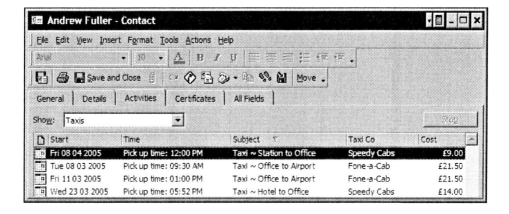

- **To enable Outlook to show items from other folders on the Activities tab of individual Contacts**:

  You must first link the other folders to the Contacts folder. This is done from the Activities tab of the Properties dialog box of the Contacts folder.

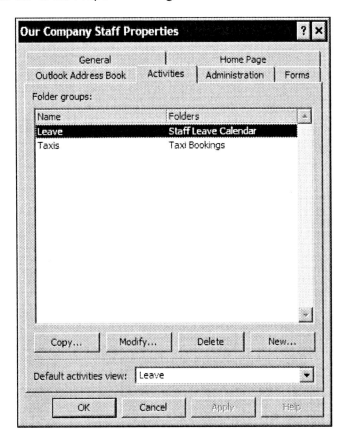

A Staff Leave Calendar

In many offices, the details of staff leave and sick leave are recorded and maintained in Excel spreadsheets or some other third-party program. It is also likely that annual leave and sick leave are also recorded as one-day events in the grey area of someone's Outlook calendar. Duplicating data in this manner takes valuable time and resources and risks error.

Depending on the level of analysis required of your leave and sick leave data, you may find that Outlook can do everything that is necessary by utilizing the following ideas, which will require entering the data only once.

If you monitor the leave and sick leave for a small number of people, you can manage staff leave in your main calendar. Each day of leave would be a one-day event and would appear in the grey area at the top of the calendar, along with any other one-day events you may have. However, if you have a large number of leave events, you can easily lose other one-day events and too many one-day events at the top of the calendar can also severely restrict your view of the rest of your calendar, as illustrated in the following screenshot:

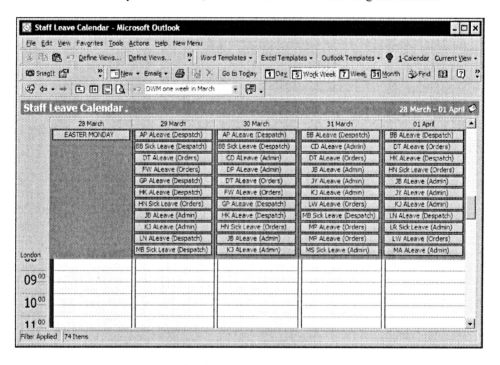

If you prefer to keep a separate calendar just for leave events, you will need to create a new calendar named, for example, Staff Leave Calendar.

The new view that we shall be creating can be for either your main calendar or a separate calendar specifically for leave. The new view will have new fields that will calculate the amount of leave taken and the number of days remaining from the entitlement and from this view we shall be able to produce leave schedules by staff member and by Department.

In preparation for creating the new view, we need to do to following:

1. Create the following categories:

CATEGORY NAME	PURPOSE
A/L	Annual leave category
S/L	Sick leave category
AF A/L (meaning: Andrew Fuller annual leave)	Annual leave category for each member of staff
AF S/L (meaning: Andrew Fuller sick leave)	Sick leave category for each member of staff
Admin	
Orders	
Despatch	
etc.	

2. As staff sick leave is reported or you are notified of staff annual leave dates, create leave events in the calendar, either as separate one-day events or over several days, but only enter the leave day events into calendar days that count as leave days i.e. working weekdays.

3. In the subject of the events, state the name or initials of the staff member and a notation to indicate whether it is annual leave or sick leave.

4. In the Location field, enter the Department where the individual works for e.g., Despatch.

5. Assign the three appropriate categories to the leave events e.g. A/L, AF A/L, Despatch. The categories in this example indicate that the event is annual leave, specifically AF's annual leave and that AF is located in the Despatch Department.

6. Ensure that there is a check in all day event and Show time as free in the calendar items.

7. If you wish to have an automatic reminder of the leave events, you should be aware that Outlook reminders fire only on events in the default calendar and not on events in a calendar that you have created yourself. This may be a consideration when deciding whether to use your main calendar or create a separate leave calendar.

8. Link the leave events in the calendar to the relevant staff contact by clicking on the Contacts button at the foot of the event window and selecting the member of staff from the Contacts folder. Ensure that you have linked the staff Contacts folder to the Staff Leave Calendar folder from the Contacts folder Properties | Activities tab and the leave events will automatically be recorded on the Activities tab of the staff Contacts files.

Creating the Calendar View

We will now create the view called Staff Annual Leave, either as a view of the main calendar or of a specific Staff Leave Calendar as follows:

1. Create a new view from the Define Views | New option and name the view Staff Annual Leave.

2. In the View Summary dialog box, click Fields, select the fields: Subject, Location, Start, and Duration, and click OK.

3. We will now create a New Field called Entitlement:

Option	Value
Name	Entitlement
Type	Number
Format	Raw

4. We will also create the following two Formula fields:

Name	In the Formula Field window
Last Day	Format ([End]- 1,"ddd dd mm yy)"
Days Remaining	([Entitlement]-([Duration]/1440)) & " Days"

5. At this point, let's check the fields in our view and rearrange them into the order shown in the following screenshot. Click OK to return to the View Summary.

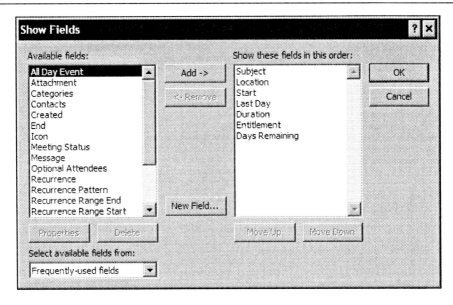

6. Continuing the design of the view, set Group By to Categories, with no check in Show field in view.

7. Set Sort items by to Start | Ascending, then by Subject | Ascending. If Outlook asks if you wish to show the End field in the view, click the No button.

8. From the Filter | More Choices | Categories option, select all the A/L categories for staff members.

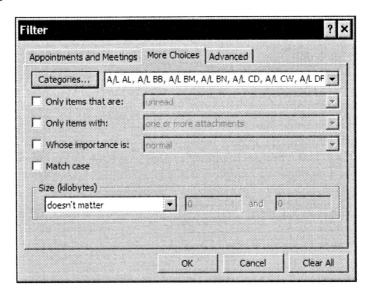

9. To restrict the records in the view to those in the current year, add a filtering criterion in the Filter | Advanced window with the following settings and then click Add to List.

Option	Value
Field	Start
Condition	Between
Value	1/1/05 and 31/12/05

10. To make the final view of the leave records easier to read, we can apply the following font settings through the Automatic Formatting option that will show leave already taken as struck out and future leave as bold.

Formatting Rule Name	Field	Condition	Value	Font Format
Future	Start	on or after	today	Bold
Past	Start	on or before	today	Strikeout

11. Exit the View Summary and from the Format Columns dialog box rename the following fields as follows:

Field name	New name
Subject	Staff Leave
Location	Department
Start	First Day

What Just Happened?

We have just created a view that can be applied to either a default calendar or a separate leave calendar that will hold the annual leave records of the members of staff in our organization and will make this detailed information available instantly and simply by switching from the Day/Week/Month view to the Staff Annual Leave view.

- To calculate the value of the Last Day field, we did not use the Outlook field End to show the last day of the event because an Outlook event is for one full day, 24 hours, from midnight to midnight. So the End field will actually show an event ending on the following day. Our new field, Last Day, will subtract one day from the end date and thereby reflect the true span of the event.

- The Format ([End- 1]) function around the calculation will format the result according to the formatting template "ddd dd mm yy" which shows the day and date without the time.

- The formula that calculates the value of the Days Remaining field divides the Duration field by 1440 before subtracting it from the Entitlement field. This is because, although the Duration field displays the length of time in days, it actually holds the time span as multiples of 24 hours in minutes. It is necessary therefore to divide Duration by the number of minutes in 24 hours, which is 1440.

To enable the calculation of the total amount of leave taken and the balance available, you will need to enter manually the number of leave entitlement days for the year into the first Entitlement field of the new leave year. Every member of staff starts the new leave year with a leave entitlement of a certain number of days. In the example overleaf, CW starts the new leave year with 25 days.

Outlook will subtract from the entitlement figure the number of days taken in the Duration field and return the balance in the Days Remaining field. As more leave events are created in the calendar and to produce a running sum, bring down the figure from the previous Days Remaining field into the next Entitlement field.

The Result

Here is the finished view of the calendar:

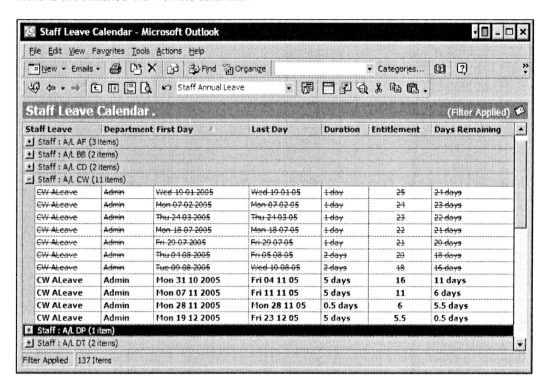

This view of the calendar can be printed, either the whole table, which would produce a schedule of leave for all staff, or only selected rows for individuals. If you wish to print individual schedules, select only the rows for the individual staff member in the view and from the File menu choose Print, or click the Print button. Click Page Setup to set the print style and to type a Header and Footer, and Preview to see the result.

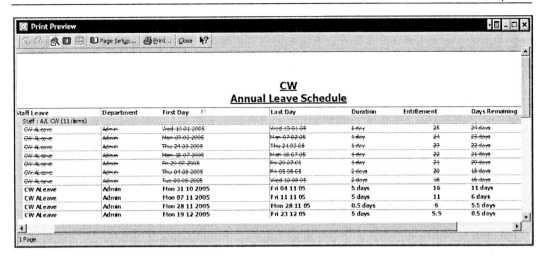

CW
Annual Leave Schedule

Staff Leave	Department	First Day	Last Day	Duration	Entitlement	Days Remaining
Staff : A/L CW (11 items)						
~~CW ALeave~~	~~Admin~~	~~Wed 19 01 2005~~	~~Wed 19 01 05~~	~~1 day~~	~~25~~	~~24 days~~
~~CW ALeave~~	~~Admin~~	~~Mon 07 02 2005~~	~~Mon 07 02 05~~	~~1 day~~	~~24~~	~~23 days~~
~~CW ALeave~~	~~Admin~~	~~Thu 24 03 2005~~	~~Thu 24 03 05~~	~~1 day~~	~~23~~	~~22 days~~
~~CW ALeave~~	~~Admin~~	~~Mon 18 07 2005~~	~~Mon 18 07 05~~	~~1 day~~	~~22~~	~~21 days~~
~~CW ALeave~~	~~Admin~~	~~Fri 29 07 2005~~	~~Fri 29 07 05~~	~~1 day~~	~~21~~	~~20 days~~
~~CW ALeave~~	~~Admin~~	~~Thu 04 08 2005~~	~~Fri 05 08 05~~	~~2 days~~	~~20~~	~~18 days~~
~~CW ALeave~~	~~Admin~~	~~Tue 09 08 2005~~	~~Wed 10 08 05~~	~~2 days~~	~~18~~	~~16 days~~
CW ALeave	**Admin**	**Mon 31 10 2005**	**Fri 04 11 05**	**5 days**	**16**	**11 days**
CW ALeave	**Admin**	**Mon 07 11 2005**	**Fri 11 11 05**	**5 days**	**11**	**6 days**
CW ALeave	**Admin**	**Mon 28 11 2005**	**Mon 28 11 05**	**0.5 days**	**6**	**5.5 days**
CW ALeave	**Admin**	**Mon 19 12 2005**	**Fri 23 12 05**	**5 days**	**5.5**	**0.5 days**

Looking at CW's leave record, we can see the results of the Automatic Formatting that we set up; past leave has been struck out and future leave is in bold.

We can also see from CW's records that on 28th November 2005 he will be taking only half a day as leave. Outlook can handle a half-day in its calculations but how was it recorded in the calendar? As has been mentioned before, in Outlook, a day is 24 hours, so to record CW's half day we have to block out 12 hours, from midday to midnight or midnight to midday that day (this would be another good reason to use a separate calendar for leave).

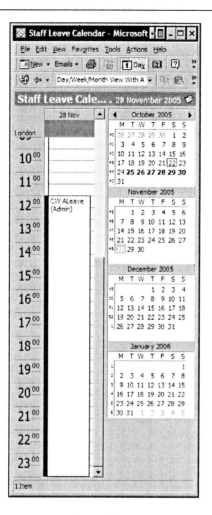

As we have linked the Leave events to the staff contacts' records, the Leave items will appear on the Activities tab of the staff members' records as illustrated opposite:

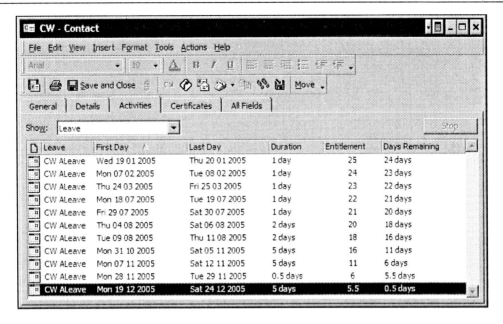

A Staff Leave Calendar—Daily View by Department

This variation on the previous technique will show daily absences by Department for a number of weeks ahead and can help in the planning of departmental staff cover.

In preparing our previous example we created Annual Leave and Sick Leave categories for each member of staff. We shall also use those categories in this view and at the filtering stage we shall select the S/L (Sick Leave) as well as the A/L (Annual Leave) categories for staff members.

Creating the Calendar View

1. Create a new view from the Define Views | New option and name the view Daily Absence by Dept, with the fields Subject and Start.

2. Set Group by to Location (which will be the departments) and then by the Start Date.

3. Set Sort Items by to Start.

4. From the Filter | More Choices | Categories option, select all of the Annual Leave and Sick Leave categories.

   To restrict the number of days shown in the view to today and two weeks from now, use the following criterion in the Advanced Filter tab:

Option	Value
Field	Start
Condition	between
Value	today and 2w

5. This criterion uses the Outlook natural language facility, **2w meaning 2 weeks**.

6. Exit the View Summary and from the Format Columns dialog box change the following fields as follows:

Field name	New name	Format
Subject	Daily Absence by Department	
Start		Date only

What Just Happened?

The view that we have just created shows annual and sick leave for the current date and two weeks ahead. The events are grouped, first by the departments in which the staff members work, and then by the dates that leave is to be taken.

Entering the events in the Day/Week/Month view of the calendar and switching to this Daily Absence by Dept view will not only give an overview of the organization's workforce, but will also allow speedy access to staff absence data and enable proactive identification of areas of staff weakness and assist with forward planning of human resources.

Each day, the first and last days shown in the view will move forward one day as the filter criterion will always determine the period from the current day and for two weeks ahead. This view allows us to see, by Department, who is on sick leave, who will be on annual leave for the next two weeks and where cover might be needed for that period.

The Result

Here is a view of the finished result:

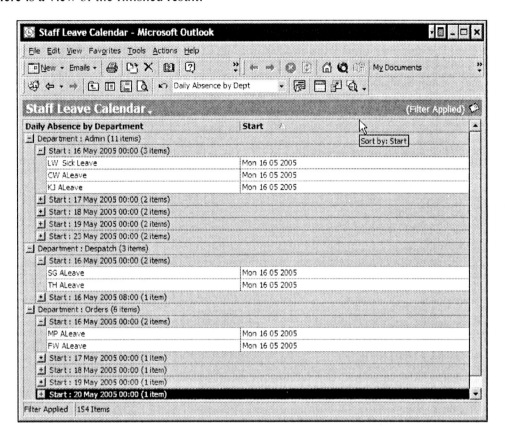

A Staff Leave Calendar—Sick Leave View

An organization's Human Resources Department may also wish to be alerted to staff sick leave that exceeds a certain number of days and Outlook can highlight sick leave incidents by applying an Automatic Formatting criterion as follows:

Creating the Calendar View

1. Create staff sick leave events in the Staff Leave Calendar and assign the sick leave categories to the events.

2. Create a new view called Sick Leave, with the fields: Subject, Location, Start, End, and Duration.

3. Continue as in the example for annual leave, except filter on the staff members' Sick Leave categories.

4. Add an Automatic Formatting rule as follows:

Formatting Rule Name	Field	Condition	Value	Font Format
>2 days	Duration	is more than	2d (meaning 2 days)	Color Red

5. Exit the View Summary and from the Format Columns dialog box rename the following fields as follows:

Field name	New name
Location	Department

What Just Happened?

When we apply the view that we have just created, the Duration field will show the number of sick leave days taken and the records where the duration exceeds 2 days will be in red font.

The Result

Here is a view of the finished result:

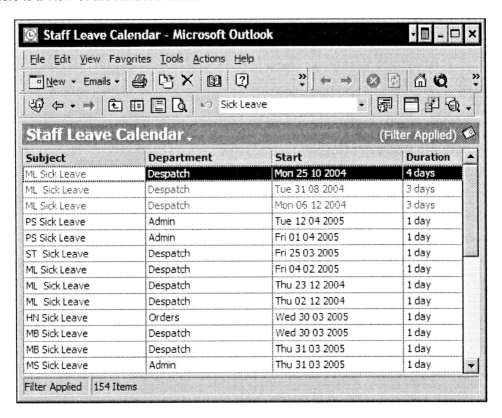

A Calendar View that Records Conference Costs

A busy Outlook calendar will contain a variety of events that may or may not have costs associated with them. For those items that incur costs, what better place to record the expenses than with the events themselves? The Day/Week/Month view will show the events in the calendar in the normal way, but by switching to a Conference Costs View, the costs and expenses associated with the event will be displayed.

Creating the Calendar View

To create a view of a calendar in which to record the cost of conferences, meetings, functions, etc. you will first need to ensure that the specific conferences in the calendar are assigned to their own categories then continue as follows:

1. Create a new view from the Define Views | New option and name the view Conference Costs.

2. In the View Summary dialog box click Fields, and select the fields: Subject and Start, and click OK.

3. We will now create two new manual fields:

Name	Type	Format	Purpose
Cost per Head	Currency	2 decimal format	The manual entry of the cost per head rate for delegates.
No of Guests	Number	All digits	The manual entry of the number of delegates that attend the event.

4. We will also create the following Formula fields:

Name	In the Formula Field window
VAT	Format([Cost per Head]*[No of Guests]*0.175,"£#0.00")
Total	Format([Cost per Head]*[No of Guests]+[VAT],"£#0.00")

5. Continuing the design of the view, set Group By to Categories, with no check in Show field in view.

6. Set Sort items by to Start | Descending.

7. From the Filter | More Choices | Categories option, select all the relevant conference categories you have created.

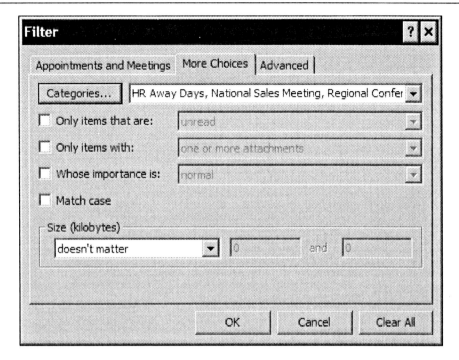

8. Exit the View Summary and from the Format Columns dialog box rename the following fields as follows:

Field name	New name	Format
Subject	Conferences	
Start	Date	Date only

What Just Happened?

We have constructed a table view of a calendar that filters only events, conferences, meetings, etc. for which we need to record the costs. Whether you are the owner or the hirer of the venue, there is no need to enter the data into another program; the records are available simply by switching views.

The fields Cost per Head and No of Guests require us to enter the basic numbers and the VAT and Total fields will execute the calculations. Until you enter figures or a zero in the Cost per Head and No of Guests fields you will find the #ERROR message in the VAT and Total fields.

The formula in the VAT field, 0.175, is VAT @ 17.5% and this can be changed to correspond with the prevailing rate. The calculation is surrounded by Format (.................,"£#0.00") to format the result as currency.

The Total field multiplies the number of delegates by the rate per head and adds the VAT value. This calculation is also surrounded by Format (.................,"£#0.00") to format the result as currency.

The Result

Here is the finished view of the calendar:

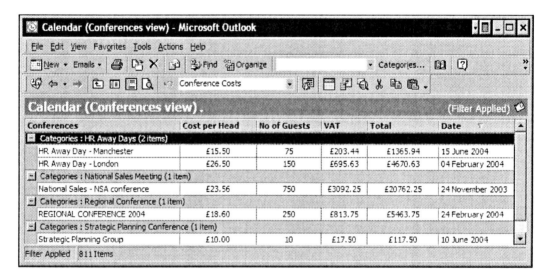

A Calendar View that Records Your Expenses

This view will provide a simple, logical and safe way to record and store your mileage and expenses. Completing your expenses claims will no longer involve storing for weeks numerous scrappy pieces of paper with hastily scribbled mileage figures. Once the expense details are entered into this view, the scrappy pieces of paper can be thrown away and the expense claim can be completed in a sane and organized fashion.

Ensure that the items in your calendar for which you will be claiming expenses are assigned to a suitable category, e.g. Expenses.

Creating the Calendar View

1. Create a new view of your calendar from the Define Views | New option and name the view My Expenses, with the following Outlook fields:

2. In the View Summary dialog box, click Fields, and select the fields: Subject and Start, and click OK.

3. We will now create the following new manual fields:

Name	Type	Format	Purpose
Hotel	Currency	2 decimal format	The manual entry of any hotel expenses
Miles	Number	All digits	The manual entry of mileage
Rail Cost	Currency	2 decimal format	The manual entry of train fare
Misc	Currency	2 decimal format	The manual entry of any miscellaneous costs

4. We will also create the following three new Formula fields:

Name	In the Formula Field window
Cost per mile	Format(0.4,"£#0.00")
Mileage Cost	Format([Miles]*[Cost per mile],"£#0.00")
Total Expenses	Format([Hotel]+[Mileage Cost]+[Rail Cost]+[Misc],"£#0.00")

5. Continuing the design of the view, set Group By to (None).

6. Set Sort items by to Start | Descending.

7. From the Filter | More Choices | Categories option, select the Expenses category.

8. Exit the View Summary and from the Format Columns dialog box rename the following fields as follows:

Field name	New name	Format
Subject	Expenses	
Start	Date	Date only

What Just Happened?

When we apply the My Expenses view to the calendar, we see a list of the events that are assigned to the Expenses category, for which we have expenses to claim, and fields representing the various types of expense. Initially some of the fields will contain #ERROR messages. These errors can be ignored as they will disappear when you start entering the data.

The Cost per mile field is storing the value of 0.4 and is formatted as currency (meaning 40p per mile). This field does not need to be in the view. Once a mileage cost is set it should not change often and it does not need to be in the view for the calculation to work. The rate can be changed by altering the figure 0.4 in the formula in the field.

The Mileage Cost field will calculate the mileage cost by multiplying the number of miles recorded in the Miles field by the cost per mile and the result will be formatted as currency.

When you enter figures in the Hotel, Misc, Rail Cost or Miles fields, the Total Expenses field will automatically add the values of all the expense fields and format the result as currency.

If there are no costs for a particular field—for example if you went by train and not by car there will be no mileage—make sure that you enter a zero where there was no cost otherwise some fields, including Total Expenses will return the #ERROR message. Empty fields must contain a zero for the calculation to complete.

The Result

Here is the finished My Expenses view of the calendar:

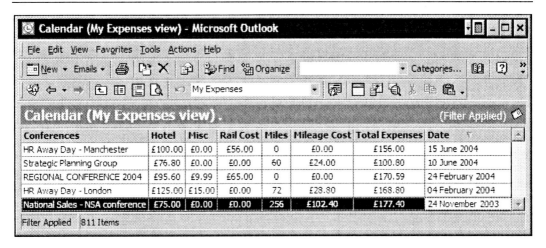

When it is time to claim your expenses, do a printout of this view and complete your claim form from the details on the printout.

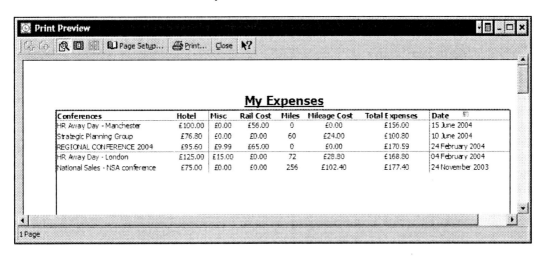

Those items not to be claimed next time can be excluded from the view by removing them from the Expenses category.

A To Do List for Calendar Items

Simply entering appointments, meetings, etc., in a calendar is very often not the end of the arrangements that need to be made for these events. For example, there will be meeting rooms to be booked, teleconferences to be arranged, papers to be prepared and circulated, travel arrangements to make, deadlines to be met, etc. So a To Do List for these associated Tasks would be useful, but instead of creating a separate To Do List, perhaps in the Tasks folder, we can utilize the information already in an Outlook Calendar to create a To Do List view of a calendar.

We can also include in the view Automatic Formatting rules that will provide a visual reminder of the priorities in the list. For example, you may wish to be alerted to items that are due today, overdue, or still to be done and this can be achieved by color-coding the filtered items.

Creating the Calendar View

In preparation for creating a To Do List view of a Calendar, you will need to create appropriate Categories for the list items like creating Categories such as Rooms to Book, Teleconferences to arrange, Reports Required, Deadlines, etc.

1. Then create a new view from the Define Views | New option and name the view To Do List.

2. In the View Summary dialog box, click Fields, and select the fields: Subject and Start, and click OK.

3. We will now create the following three new manual fields:

Name	Type	Format	Purpose
Action	Text	Text	A brief description of an action that has to be performed in connection with the calendar item.
Deadline	Date/Time	A date-only format	A deadline date that you set yourself for the Action.
Done?	Yes/No	Yes/No format	This field, when clicked, will cycle between Yes and No and will be the trigger for the Automatic Formatting rules that we shall create.

4. Continuing the design of the view, set Group By to Categories, with no check in Show field in view.

5. Set Sort items by to Start | Descending.

6. From the Filter | More Choices | Categories option, select all the relevant To Do List categories that you have created.

7. From the Automatic Formatting option, click Add, and create the following three rules:

Formatting Rule Name	Field	Condition	Value	Font Format	Purpose
Completed	Done?	equals	Yes	Strikeout	Strikeout those items where the Done? field reads Yes.
Deadline Today	Start	today		Blue Italics	Color blue and italicize items when the date in the Deadline field is the current date.
Overdue	Done?	equals	No	Red	Color red those items where the Done? field reads
	Deadline	on or before	Yesterday		No and the date in the Deadline field is on or before the current date.

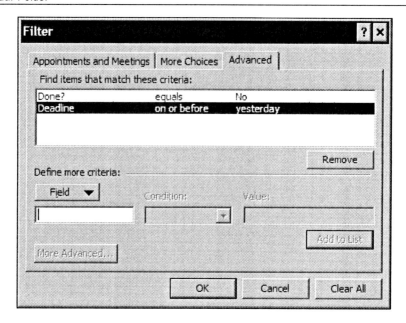

8. Exit the View Summary and from the Format Columns dialog box rename the following fields as follows:

Field name	New name	Format
Subject	To Do List	
Start	Meeting Date	Date only

What Just Happened?

We have just created a table-type view that will filter items in the calendar that require certain actions or preparation. The type of action or preparation is reflected in the category name to which the items have been assigned. The view then groups items by category, so when we apply the view we have a neat list of items listed under the necessary actions.

In the To Do List view of your calendar you can then enter Deadline dates in the Deadline field and when an item has been completed, click into the Done? field, to create a Yes or No.

The Result

Here is the finished view of the calendar:

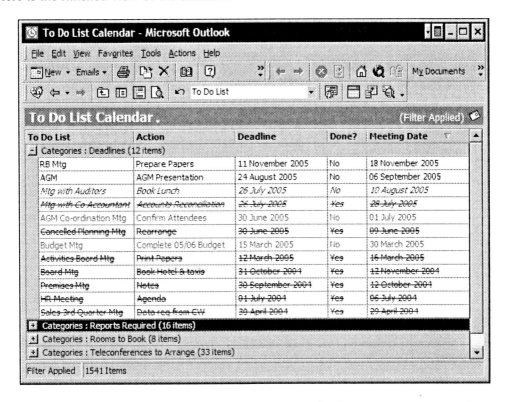

The item Mtg with Auditors with the action Book Lunch in the Deadlines category has a Deadline date of 26th July 2005 and as the current date in this instance is 26th July 2005, the item is formatted in blue italics. Deadlines that have been missed are in red and actions that have been completed are struck out.

The To Do List can also be printed in its entirety or only selected items or Categories as an aide memoir.

Summary

In this chapter we have added extra dimensions to Outlook Calendars by uncovering some rather interesting ways to customize the views.

We can now manipulate Outlook to provide instant answers to any number of questions concerning the calendars that we manage. We have seen how we can store detailed information directly into calendar entries that can then be presented and printed in professional formats for individual or management use; information relating to staff leave, appointments and meetings, expenses, etc.

The examples given in this chapter are just a few illustrations of what Outlook can do and we are sure that now that you are aware of these features, you will be able devise powerful permutations that match your needs and those of your organization.

In the next chapter we shall apply similar and new techniques to Contacts folders that will revolutionize the way you think of Outlook Contacts.

2

The Contacts Folder

The conventional use of the Contacts folder is to store the details of people with whom you communicate. However, with a little imagination, Contacts folders can be used to store and manipulate the details of almost anything.

In this chapter, we will look at the following examples of useful, unusual, and practical customizations of conventional Outlook contact data:

- A table of Distribution Lists that displays the dates on which they were created
- A Business Directory of Suppliers
- A Staff Contacts folder that calculates length of service and leave entitlement
- A Contacts folder for Company Vehicles

A Distribution Lists View

Distribution Lists are created to make it easy to send one email to several recipients. These recipients would all have a common interest in the email that you are sending and are often therefore members of specific groups, regular meetings, committees, etc. But these groups can have finite life spans and you can find that you accumulate Distribution Lists that are out of date and defunct. To assist in identifying the current validity of your Distribution Lists, we will create a view of your Contacts folder showing the dates on which the Distribution Lists were created.

If you have a large number of Distribution Lists, you could either create a separate Contacts folder to store only Distribution Lists or use a view of your main Contacts folder that filters Distribution Lists. As Outlook does not provide a predefined view for Distribution Lists, the following custom view not only filters Distributions Lists but also includes the Created field to show the date on which each list was created, which will enable you to identify which lists may be deleted.

Creating the Contacts View

1. Create a new table-type view from the Define Views | New option and name the view Distribution Lists.

2. In the View Summary dialog box, click Fields and select the fields: Full Name and Created, and click OK.

3. We will now add a new manual field as follows:

Name	Type	Format	Purpose
Members	Text	Text	To enter the names of the members of the list

4. Set Group By to (none).

5. Set Sort items by to File As | Ascending.

6. From the Filter | Advanced tab create the following filter:

Field	Condition	Value
Message Class (from the All Mail fields list)	is (exactly)	IPM.DistList

7. From the Other Settings option, click Allow in-cell editing.

What Just Happened?

We have constructed a view of a Contacts folder that will permit you to see all your distribution lists together. It will also enable you to identify and weed out those lists that you no longer use, or to find a list quickly according to when it was created, which is likely to be around the time that the group formed.

The view also contains a custom field named Members. Unfortunately, Outlook does not provide a way to show, automatically, the names of the members of a distribution list. This Members field is a text field and would require that you enter manually the names of the list members into this field.

The Result

Here is the view we have just created:

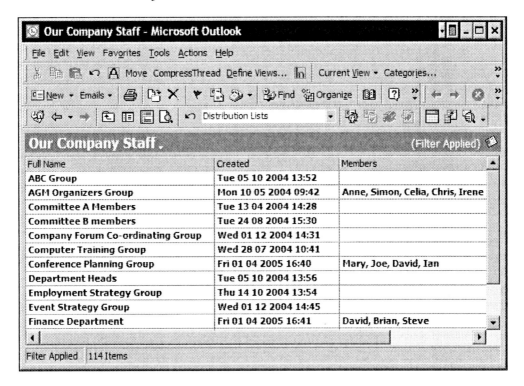

Another Contacts list that would benefit from a firm and organized structure is that of suppliers of goods or services. We will now create a Contacts folder and view that will produce a well-organized business directory.

A View of Suppliers of Goods or Services

We will begin with creating the Contacts view.

Creating the Contacts View

1. Create a Contacts folder specifically for the details of your contacts at companies that supply goods or services, named Suppliers.

2. Create Categories for your supplier companies that describe, in general terms, their trade or profession. For example, Architects, Lawyers, Building Supplies, etc.

3. Create a new table-type view from the Define Views | New option and name the view Business Directory.

4. In the View Summary dialog box, click Fields, and select the fields: Company, Full Name, Email, Country/Region, Business Phone, Business Fax, and Mobile Phone, and click OK.

5. Create a new manual field as follows:

Field	Type	Format	Purpose
Commodity	Text	Text	To record the specific commodities or services that each supplier provides, e.g. Category = Architects, Commodity = Major Projects > 10m

6. Set Group By to Categories and then by Commodity.

What Just Happened?

Outlook does not allow us to group by more than one category, but we have been able to produce the same effect by first grouping by the Category field, which is the first level description of the trade or profession and then by the Commodity field that describes the uniqueness of the supplier within the category.

This will enable you to identify, and locate quickly, the contact details of the specific suppliers to match your exact need.

The Result

The result is a well-organized Business Directory:

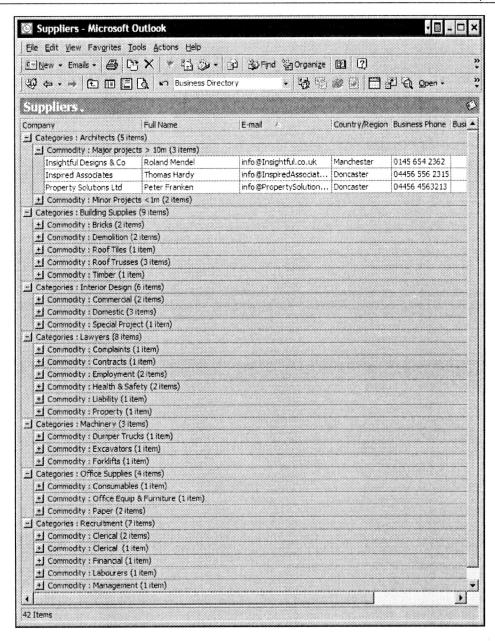

Creating Views of Staff Data

When you are constructing a new view, you may find that too many fields result in the viewing area being cramped and data not being easily visible. In this case, consider combining related fields into one new field. For example, you may want to include the contact details of the next of kin in your view of staff data, in which case, create a new combination field as follows:

Option	Value
Name	Next of Kin
Type	Combination
Formula	Edit
Fields	[Spouse] ~ [Home Phone]

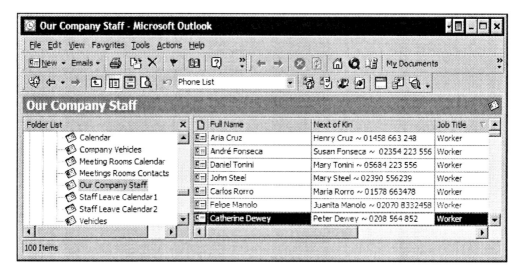

There is a vast amount of information that can be held about staff that would be useful to store in one place, and Outlook can be that place. Outlook can store not only contact information, but also information about the company equipment that is issued to staff members e.g. mobile phones, laptops, and cars; about staff length of service and leave entitlement; about training and courses attended; about salary progression, commission and bonuses, etc.

The examples we will now work through relate to other areas of a business that need to be managed and where Outlook can assist a small business, such as employees' length of service and company vehicles.

A Length of Service and Leave Entitlement View

We will now describe how to create a new view of a Contacts Folder called Length of Service that will show the length of service and the amount of leave that each staff member is entitled to. This information will enable us to enter the correct leave entitlement into the Entitlement field in the Staff Leave calendar that we created in the last chapter.

The following view should be created in the Contacts folder that contains staff data and the view utilizes the details of a company policy that allows staff members the following numbers of days leave depending on their length of service:

No of years service	No of days leave
10 years or more	30 days
5 years or more	25 days
Less than 5 years	22 days

Creating the Contacts View

1. Create a new table-type view from the Define Views | New option and name the view Length of Service.

2. In the View Summary dialog box, click Fields, and select the fields: Full Name, and Job Title, and click OK.

3. We will now create a new field for the manual entry of the date on which staff members join the company: We will name the field Starting Date, its type will be Date/Time, and its format will be a date-only format.

4. We will also create the following new formula fields of which only two will be shown in the view. The three fields not to be shown in the view are required to support the final calculations.
    The abbreviation LOS means Length of Service.

Name	In the Formula Field window	To be Shown in the View?
LOS mnths	DateDiff("m",[Starting Date],Date())	NO
LOS yrs	Int([LOS mnths]/12)	NO
LOS M Diff	[LOS mnths]-([LOS yrs]*12)	NO

Name	In the Formula Field window	To be Shown in the View?
Length of Service	[LOS yrs] & " yr(s) " & [LOS M Diff] & " mnth(s)"	YES
Leave Entitlement	IIf((([LOS yrs]>=10),"30",IIf(([LOS yrs]>=5,"25","22")) & " days"	YES

What Just Happened?

We have created a view of a staff Contacts folder that has six new fields, three of which provide background calculations and do not appear in the view.

- The LOS mnths field calculates the difference in months ("m") between the Starting Date and the current date.

- The LOS yrs field returns the integer of the LOS mnths field divided by 12.

- The LOS M Diff field calculates the difference in months between the number of months in the LOS mnths field and the equivalent number of months in the LOS yrs field.

- The Length of Service field concatenates the LOS yrs and LOS M Diff fields and adds the text yr(s) and mnth(s).

- Finally, the Leave Entitlement field tests the number of years in the LOS yrs field; if it is equal to or greater than 10 the field will return 30, if the number is equal to or greater than 5 the field will return 25, otherwise (i.e. when LOS yrs is less than 5) the field will return 22.

The Result

The screenshot opposite shows all the fields that we have just created, but all that are necessary in the view are Full Name, Job Title, Starting Date, Length of Service, and Leave Entitlement:

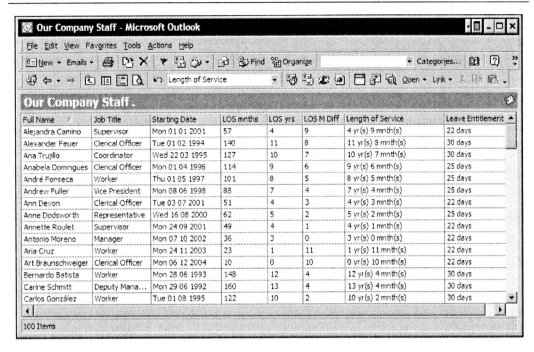

Adding Details of Company Vehicles

An organization that has a fleet of vehicles may allocate those vehicles to staff according to their job titles. By including the following formula field into a view of a staff Contacts folder, Outlook can indicate which members of staff are eligible for company vehicles.

Create the new Formula field as follows:

Name	In the Formula Field window
Co car?	IIf([Job Title]="President","yes",IIf([Job Title]="Vice President","yes",IIf([Job Title]="Manager","yes",IIf([Job Title]="Representative","yes",""))))

This formula is testing the Job Title field to see if the title is President, Vice President, Manager, or Representative. In this particular company, only these four titles are entitled to a company car. If the Job Title field contains one of these titles, the Co car? field will return the word yes; otherwise the field will be blank, which is created by the double quotes ("") at the very end of the formula.

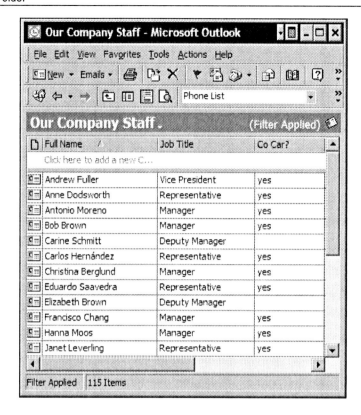

A Contacts Folder for Company Vehicles

Let's now take a real leap of imagination and consider that if our company has a fleet of vehicles, why can't we store the details in a Contacts folder? These details could include the make, model, year of manufacture, registration number, mileage, and date of service; perhaps we could even get Outlook to remind us when the vehicles should be serviced.

This amount of very specific data would need to be held in a separate Contacts folder. So the first action would be to create a new suitably named Contacts folder, not for people but for company cars.

Creating the Contacts View

Rather than modify an existing view, create a new view as follows:

1. Create a new table type view from the Define Views | New option and name the view Company Vehicles.

2. In the View Summary dialog box, click Fields, and select the fields: Full Name, Birthday, and Contacts and click OK.

3. We will now create the following five new manual fields:

Name	Type	Format	Purpose
Make and Model	Text	Text	To enter the make and model of the vehicle
Year	Number	Raw	To enter the year of manufacture
Previous mileage	Number	All digits	To enter the previous mileage
Current Mileage	Number	All digits	To enter the current mileage
Last Service	Date/Time	Date only	To enter the date that the vehicle was last serviced

4. We will also create the following two new Formula fields:

Name	In the Formula Field window
5000m Service	IIf([Current Mileage]-[Previous Mileage]>5000,"DUE!","")
6mnthly Service	IIf([Last Service]="None","Last Service?",IIf(Date()-[Last Service]>180,"DUE!"))

5. From the Format Columns dialog box, rename the following fields:

Field name	New name
Full Name	Reg No
Birthday	Service Date
Contacts	Current User

What Just Happened?

We have created a view for entering the basic descriptions of vehicles plus the mileage and service details. Vehicle servicing may depend upon the mileage a vehicle does or the time period between services, or both.

The registration numbers of the vehicles will be entered into the Reg No field and the other details into the other custom fields. The Birthday field (renamed Service Date) is being used because, when we click into this field, Outlook will bring up a calendar from which to pick the date and, when a date has been chosen, Outlook will automatically make an entry in the default calendar and create a reminder for this item. A possible disadvantage is that Outlook will create a recurring annual event. This may not be what we want if vehicles require servicing more frequently than annually and the vehicle service event will appear like this in your calendar:

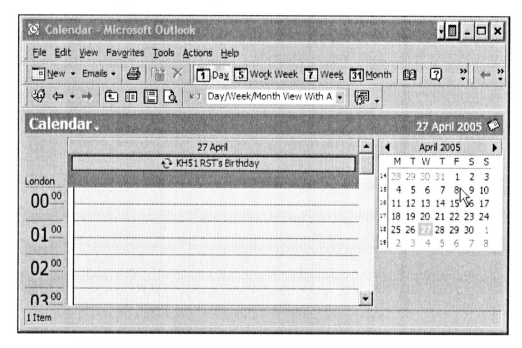

However, you can open the event, change the word Birthday to Service, remove the recurrence and Save and Close.

The formula fields 5000m Service and 6mnthly Service will take information from the servicing data in other fields and will return reminder comments depending upon the criteria set in the formula.

For example:

1. The 5000m Service field:

    If the difference between the current and the previous mileage for the vehicles is greater than 5000 (or any mileage figure a company wishes to use for servicing its fleet) then the field will return the word DUE! otherwise it will be blank ("").

2. The 6mnthly Service field:

    There are two parts to this formula, the first part is saying:

    o   If there is no date in the Last Service field, return the words Last Service? or whatever words you choose that alert you to the fact that the vehicle hasn't been serviced or that you haven't entered a date in the Last Service field.

    o   If today's date minus the Last Service date is greater than 180 days—in other words, if it is longer than 6 months since the last service, the field will return the word DUE!.

The Result

As you enter the vehicle details, your company vehicle records will begin to look like this:

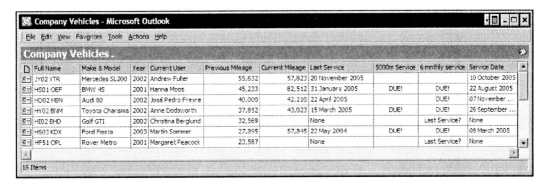

The first vehicle has not done 5000 miles since the previous reading and its last service was less than 6 months ago so there are no warning messages in this record.

The third vehicle has exceeded its 6 monthly service.

The second and fourth vehicles have exceeded both limits and Outlook is telling us very clearly that the service is due.

Services have been booked for all Vehicles except vehicles Reg Nos HI02 BHD and HF51 OPL.

We have also linked the vehicles' records to the current users by clicking on the Contacts button at the foot of the vehicles' Contacts records and the staff names appear in the Contacts field, renamed Current User.

The link is reciprocal, so that by linking the vehicle record to a staff member, the staff member will appear in the Contacts box at the foot of the vehicle record and the vehicle registration number will appear in the Contacts box at the foot of the staff member's record.

Each will also appear on the Activities tab of the Contacts record of the other.

When we click on the Activities tab of the record of Anne Dodsworth, the vehicle is listed there and we can add more fields from the Field Chooser dialog box to show a full record of the vehicle she currently uses.

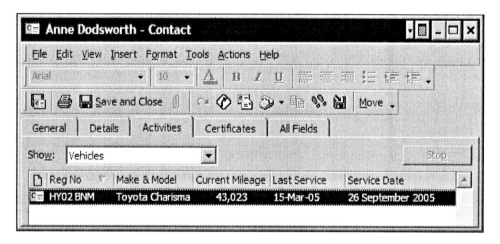

Similarly, if we look at the contact record of the vehicle HY02 BNM:

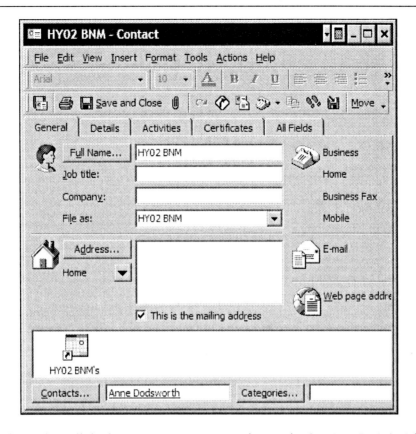

The vehicle has been linked to Anne Dodsworth and even the Service (Birthday) is automatically inserted into the contact record of the vehicle, enabling us to double-click the link to see the details of the service booking.

The Activities tab for the vehicle HY02 BNM shows the current user of the vehicle and their details.

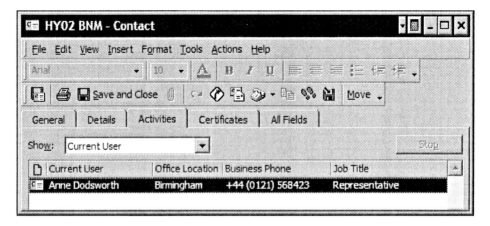

Summary

We have so far explored some unusual uses for the Outlook Calendar and some extraordinary ways to manipulate the Contacts folder. Hopefully by now you are beginning to sense that we have been gathering together the ingredients and the techniques that are the building blocks that will shape the unique solutions in the final chapter. The next building block is Tasks and we shall be exploring ways to utilize Tasks in the next chapter.

3
The Tasks Folder

A simple definition of an **Outlook Task** is that it is a personal or work-related job or assignment whose progress can be tracked to completion. It is an activity that may have a completion date and current status.

However, it is not quite as simple as that, as there are three types of Outlook Task and for each task there are three levels of priority and five stages of progress.

The three types of task that you can have in your Tasks folder, at any one time are:

- A task created by you and assigned to someone else

- A task created by someone else and assigned to you

- A task created by you for your own benefit

Each type of task has a different icon but, even if you include the fields Requested By, Assigned, and Owner in the folder view, it is still not easy to distinguish, and therefore manage, the different types of task.

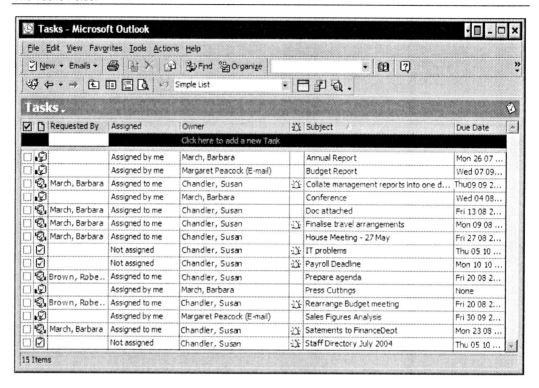

Each task can have priority settings of Low, Normal, or High and be at one of the following stages: Not Started, In Progress, Waiting on Someone Else, Deferred, or Completed. The initiator of the task sets the priority level and the owner determines the progress or status levels. Both are set from within the tasks themselves as shown below:

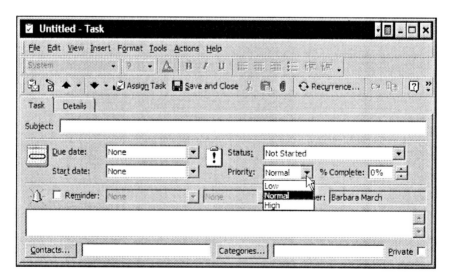

For Outlook to be able to re-grade tasks automatically through the five progress stages when they are updated, tasks must reside in the default Tasks folder. Tasks must also reside in the default Tasks folder for reminders to fire. So, in order to manage our tasks and retain the use of these important features, we must create appropriate views of the default task folder rather than create new Tasks folders.

Customizing Tasks Folder Views

Perhaps the first custom views that we should create for the default Tasks folder are those that filter the three types of Assignment, separately.

1. There is a predefined view in Outlook named Assignment and the filter condition for this view is as follows:

Field	Condition	Value
Assigned	equals	Assigned by me

It would be helpful if the name of the view could reflect the fact that it is filtering tasks created by you and assigned to someone else, and the only way to achieve that is to copy the view and rename the copy Assigned by me.

2. We can then create another copy of the Assignment view, rename it Assigned to me and change the filter condition to:

Field	Condition	Value
Assigned	equals	Assigned to me

3. For the third type of task, one created by you and for you, create a third copy of the Assignment view, rename it My Tasks, and change the filter condition to:

Field	Condition	Value
Assigned	equals	Not Assigned

The alternative to creating these three new views of the Tasks folder is to create three separate categories for the different types of assignment and group the view by Category. That way, all tasks can be seen together in the same view but grouped separately according to their assignment. The disadvantage of using this approach would be that no further category grouping or grouping by a keyword-type field would be possible, as

Outlook does not permit sub-category grouping. The way around this would be to create a new text-type field that contains a category keyword. Outlook will allow sub-grouping on a text-type field.

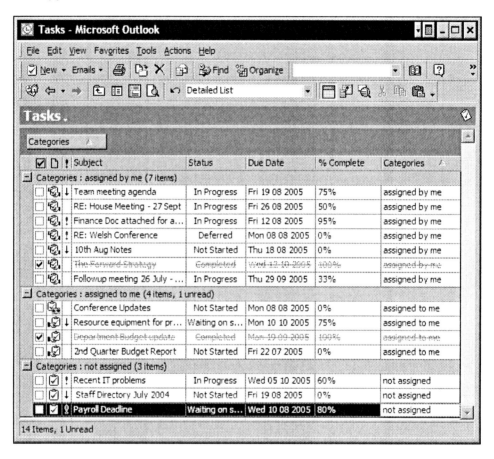

However, creating views that separate tasks by the different assignment types allows us the flexibility to use specific fields and create new fields that are appropriate to one type of task and not the others, for example:

The Assigned to Me View

1. We will add the field Requested By but stipulate that the field is not to be shown in the view but that the items are to be grouped by this field. We shall then create the following new manual field:

Name	Type	Format	Purpose
Notes to Myself	Text	Text	To write a few words to yourself about the task

2. Set Group By to Requested By.

3. From the Other Settings option, select the following:

Area	Select	Purpose
Rows	In-cell editing	To enter text into the Notes to Myself field
Auto Preview	Preview all items	To see the task details in the preview pane

The Result

This is the finished view of Tasks assigned to me:

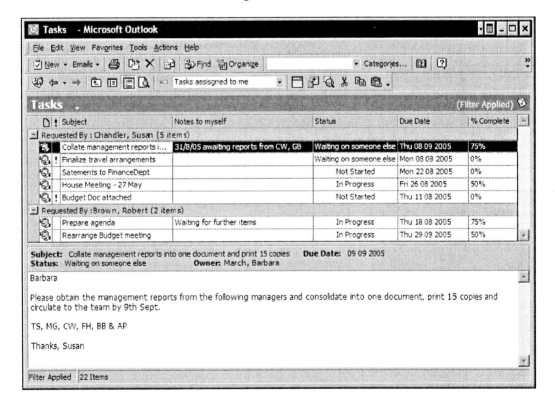

The Assigned by Me View

The Assigned by me view will need to be sorted and grouped differently. We no longer need to see the Requested By field as the tasks will have been requested by us, but we would like to see to whom we assigned the tasks i.e. the current owners of the tasks.

1. We will add to this view the field Owner and stipulate that the field is not to be shown in the view.

2. Set Group By to Owner.

The Result

This is the finished view of Tasks assigned by me:

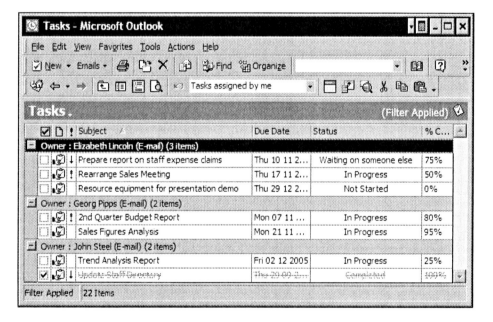

Tasks Assigned by Me View

A useful adaptation to the Assigned by me view in particular, is the ability to create a overview and evaluation of tasks by recording the length of time tasks have taken to complete, which tasks were undertaken by teams, and the roles of the assignees.

1. When you create and assign a task, enter your estimation of the time necessary for the completion of the task into the Total work field on the Details tab and instruct the assignee to enter the actual amount of time taken in the Actual work field.

2. We will add to the view the fields: Total work, Actual work, Team Task, and Role.

3. We will also add a new Formula field:

Name	In the Formula Field window
Overtime	IIf(([Actual Work]-[Total Work])/60<=0,"",(([Actual Work]-[Total Work])/60) & " hr(s)")

The Result

This is the Assigned by me view with time evaluation fields added and we can see those tasks that have exceeded our estimation of their duration by the figure in the Overtime column.

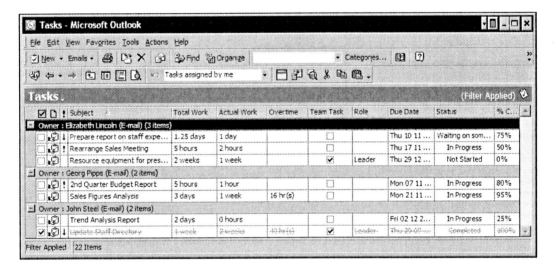

The My Tasks View

The My Tasks view will filter tasks that you set yourself and that are in your default Tasks folder because you want Outlook to remind you of them.

Creating the View

1. Create a new table type view from the Define Views | New option and name the view My Tasks.

2. In the View Summary dialog box, click Fields and select the fields: Icon, Attachment, Complete, Recurring, Subject, Reminder, and Due Date, and click OK.

3. From the Other Settings option, check Show Preview Pane. In Outlook 2003, check Preview all items and choose where to place the Reading Pane. This will enable you to see the notes you made when you created the task or, if the task was created from an email, the body text of the email.

What Just Happened?

In order to utilize the Outlook Tasks updating and reminder functions, tasks must be kept in the default Tasks folder and with the different types of task, the Tasks folder can look pretty messy and difficult to manage. But we have just created three views of the default folder that filter the three types of task separately.

We have organized the two types of assigned tasks:

- By the people who are going to be demanding results from us

- By the people that we are looking to, to produce results

We have also added a time-management Formula field to the Assigned by Me view that will enable us to monitor the time taken for the tasks. The steps for this formula are:

1. Calculate the excess time taken on a task by subtracting Total Work from Actual Work and divide by 60. The division by 60 is necessary because the time values in these two fields are held as minutes and we require the time to be expressed as hours.

2. Negative results indicate that Actual Work is less than Total Work meaning that the task was completed within the estimate. Zero results mean that the time taken matches our estimate. We don't need to see the zero or negative results, so where the results are less than or equal to zero (<=0), the formula will return a blank ("").

3. If the result does not meet either criterion, i.e. if Actual Work exceeds Total Work, the formula will return the excess time taken, expressed as hours.

The My Tasks view filters those tasks you set yourself and for which you set a reminder.

Finally, all three views would benefit from adding a second filter criterion that filters out completed tasks, for example:

Field	Condition	Value
Assigned	equals	Assigned by me / Assigned to me / Not assigned
Complete	equals	No

The Result

The finished My Tasks view below, which also shows the preview of a recurring task, has been created in Outlook 2000; there will be differences according to the version of Outlook you are using.

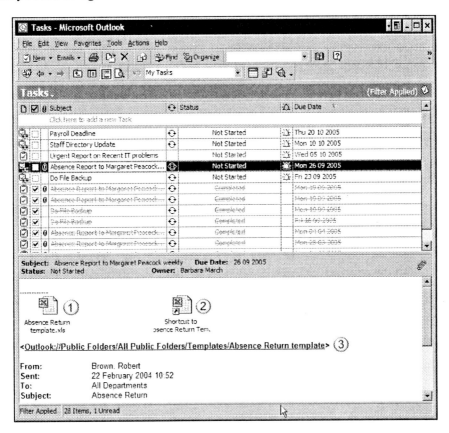

The preview area illustrates three ways to associate a file to the task:

1. Attach the file.

2. Add a shortcut to the file, or

3. Add a link to the Exchange Public folder, Templates, where the file is saved.

All except one of these tasks is a recurring task and all the current tasks have reminders set. The bell image will appear in the reminder field where tasks are not Complete and where reminders have been set.

Number of Days Left to Complete a Task

A useful new field for all of these views is one that will calculate the numbers of days that remain to complete a task. The calculation relies upon the creator of the task stipulating a due date. Where no due date is set, #ERROR will appear in the field that we are about to create.

Creating the Task

1. Create a new field as follows:

Name	In the Formula Field window
Days Remaining	Int([Due Date]-Now()) & " day(s)"

2. In the View Summary dialog box, click Automatic Formatting and turn on the standard Overdue Tasks rule that will format in red font those tasks that have not been completed by the Due Date.

The Result

This is the Tasks assigned by me view including the Days Remaining field:

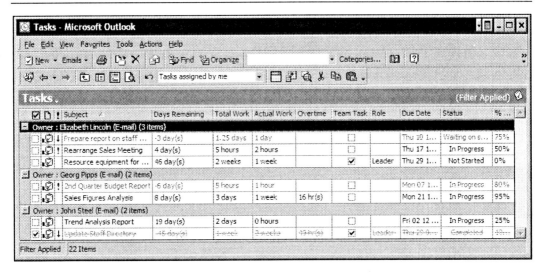

Linking Tasks to Contacts

We have seen in previous chapters the value of linking items to Contacts, and the great thing about assigned tasks is that Outlook automatically links them to the relevant contacts in your default Contacts folder.

For Tasks assigned by me, Outlook automatically places a link to the assignee's contact record in the Contacts box at the foot of the task window and double-clicking on this link will open the assignee's contact record.

The tasks will also appear on the Activities tab of the assignee's contact record and the same fields can be included on this page as they appear in the view. This produces a history of past and current tasks assigned to an individual with associated time-management data.

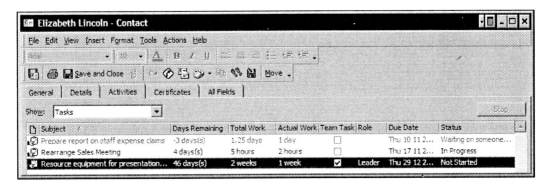

Completed Assigned Tasks

It's great when tasks are finished; we can mark them complete and get rid of them by filtering them out of a view or deleting them. However, in our haste, we may be erasing some valuable information that is still useful.

Creating Tasks for a Workshop

Take for example a car mechanic's workshop. Vehicles are brought into the workshop with a variety of problems and the administrator allocates the jobs to the mechanics in the form of Outlook Tasks. The current tasks remain in the administrator's default Tasks folder so that they can be updated by the mechanics as the jobs progress to completion. When the jobs are complete, the administrator does not delete the tasks but instead moves them into another folder especially for completed tasks.

This administrator's default Tasks folder may look something like this:

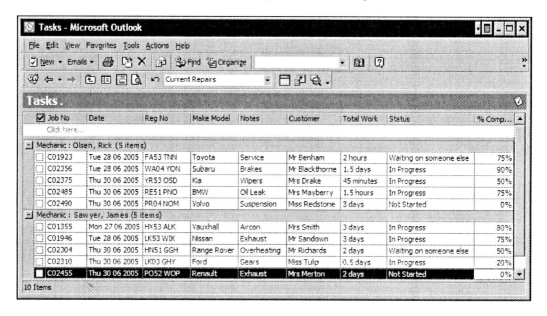

This view was created as follows:

1. From Define | Views, select the Outlook predefined view Assignment, create a copy, and name the copy Current Repairs.

2. In the View Summary dialog box, click Fields, and select the fields: Icon, Created, Owner, Subject, Contacts, Notes, Total Work, Status, and % Complete, and click OK.

3. We will now create the following two new manual fields:

Name	Type	Format	Purpose
Job No	Text	Text	To enter a job ID number
Make Model	Text	Text	To enter further vehicle identification details

4. Exit the View Summary and from the Format Columns dialog box rename the following fields as shown:

Field name	New name	Format
Owner	Mechanic	
Created	Date	Day and date only (being the date the task was created)
Subject	Reg No	
Contacts	Customer	

5. Return to View Summary and set Group by to Owner and stipulate not to show the field in the view.

What Just Happened?

Because the administrator is assigning tasks to a crew of mechanics and requires automatic updating of tasks, we have just constructed a view of the default Tasks folder that filters tasks Assigned by me. The tasks have been grouped by the owners of the tasks, i.e. the mechanics, so that their individual workload and their progression through it are easily viewable.

The administrator assesses the time necessary to complete the task and enters this estimate in the Total Work field on the Details tab of the task.

> In Outlook, the number of hours in a working day and week is set from Tools | Options | Advanced Options | Task working hours per day and Task working hours per week. Or in Outlook 2003 Tools | Options | Other | Advanced | Options | Task working hours per day and Task working hours per week.
>
> The default number of working hours per day is 8 hrs, so, if you enter 4 h (4 hours) in either the Total Work or Actual Work fields, Outlook will change that to 0.5 days.

The administrator also links the tasks to the relevant customers whose details are held as contacts in the Contacts folder. When the work is finished, the mechanic enters the actual time taken for the work in the Actual Work field and marks the task complete. The corresponding task in the administrator's default Tasks folder will be updated to show a check in the Complete icon and the task will be struck through.

The task may be complete, but it still holds valuable information that can be used for billing purposes and for management analysis.

Completed Tasks

Once tasks are complete there is no need to keep them in the default Tasks folder any longer, so, to hold completed tasks for further manipulation, we shall create a subfolder of the default Tasks folder named !Completed Vehicle Repair Tasks.

> Creating a subfolder of the default Tasks folder ensures that user-defined fields created in the higher-level folder will also be available to the subfolder.

The !Completed Vehicle Repair Tasks folder will have two new views: one named Completed Repairs and the second named Completion Time Analysis.

The Completed Repairs View

This view will calculate the cost of the repairs undertaken.

1. Create a new view from the Define Views | New option and name the view Completed Repairs.

2. In the View Summary dialog box, click Fields, and select the fields: Icon, Created, Subject, Notes, Contacts, and Actual Work from the All Tasks field list and Job No and Make Model from the User-defined fields in folder list and click OK.

3. We will now create three new manual fields:

Name	Type	Format	Purpose
Parts	Currency	2 decimal format	The manual entry of the cost of parts used
Misc	Currency	2 decimal format	The manual entry of miscellaneous costs
Paid	Currency	2 decimal format	The manual entry of amount paid

4. We will also create the following three formula fields:

Name	In the Formula Field window
Labor Cost	Format((([Actual Work]/60)*35,"currency")
VAT	Format((([Labor Cost]+[Parts]+[Misc])*0.175,"currency")
Total Cost	Format(([Labor Cost]+[Parts]+[Misc]+[VAT],"currency")

5. Continuing the design of the view, set Group by to Owner and stipulate not to show the field in the view.

6. Set Sort items by to Job No | Ascending.

7. From the Automatic Formatting option, click Add, and create the following rule:

Formatting Rule Name	Field	Condition	Value	Font Format	Purpose
Unpaid	Paid	Equals	0	Red	Use red font for unpaid items

8. Exit the View Summary and from the Format Columns dialog box rename the following fields as follows:

Field name	New name	Format
Owner	Mechanic	
Created	Date	Date only (being the date the task was created)
Subject	Reg No	

What Just Happened?

We have utilized completed tasks to store task information at source thus avoiding errors in transposing the data to another system or program. This will enable us to bill customers more timely and accurately.

The formulas at work here are:

1. The Labor Cost field, which is taking the actual time taken for the task, i.e. Actual Work, and is first dividing the number of minutes held in this field by 60 to obtain the number of hours and is then multiplying by the hourly labor rate, in this case £35 per hour. The whole calculation is surrounded by the Format function to format the result as Currency.

2. The VAT field adds the values in the fields Labor Cost, Parts, and Misc and multiplies the result by 0.175 being the VAT rate @ 17.5%. Again the final figure is formatted as Currency.

3. The Total Cost field finally adds the Labor Cost, Parts, Misc, and VAT fields together and formats the result as Currency.

The Completed Repairs View also contains an automatic formatting rule that will apply a red font to records where the Paid field equals zero.

The Result

Following is the finished view of the !Completed Vehicle Repair Tasks folder:

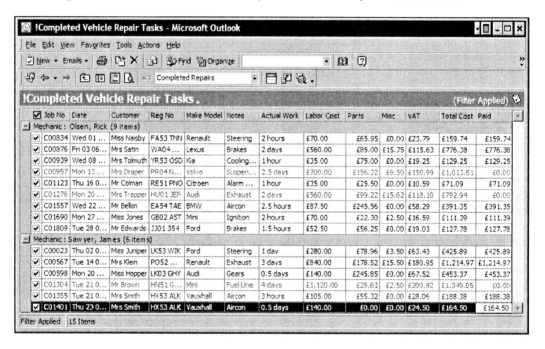

Having linked the vehicle repair tasks to customers in the Contacts folder, the administrator can also look up a customer's complete repair history on the Activities tab of their Contacts record.

The contact record in the screenshot opposite has captured vehicle repairs for customer Smith from the current repair tasks in the default Tasks folder and the completed repair tasks in its subfolder, !Completed Vehicle Repair Tasks.

The Activities tab of the Contacts record also allows grouping and these tasks have been grouped by the Complete field, so that past repairs are shown as Complete : Yes, and current repairs are Complete : No. The effects of the Automatic Formatting rule can also be seen by the formatting in red font of the current repair, which is so far incomplete, and therefore unpaid.

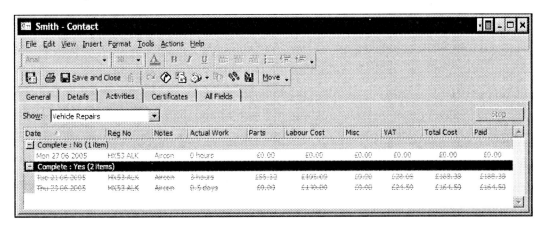

Filtering the View of Completed Repairs

If customer, Mrs. Smith, should request a statement of all the work done to her vehicle, we could construct a specific view of the Completed Vehicle Repair Tasks folder that filters only tasks for Smith.

1. Create a new view from the Define Views | New option and name the view Mrs. Smith Summary.

2. In the View Summary dialog box, click Fields, and select the fields: Created, Subject, Notes, and Actual Work from the All Tasks field list and Job No, Make Model, Labor Cost, Parts, Misc, VAT, Total Cost, and Paid from the User-defined fields in folder list.

3. From the Filter | Advanced tab create the following filter:

Field	Condition	Value
Contacts	contains	Smith

4. Exit the View Summary and from the Format Columns dialog box rename the following fields as shown:

Field name	New name	Format
Created	Date	Date only (being the date the task was created)
Subject	Reg No	

5. Apply the view to the folder and preview the print from File | Print Preview.

6. From Page Setup | Header | Footer tab, enter a heading for the printout, plus date etc. in the footer.

The Result

The result, when printed on company headed paper will produce a perfectly acceptable statement for Mrs. Smith.

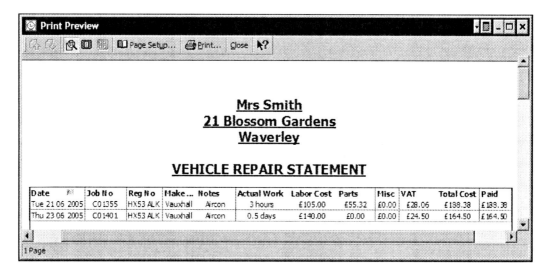

The Completion Time Analysis View

Another use for the completed tasks records of this car mechanics' workshop is in time analysis, something that the management might like to exploit.

The second view of the Completed Vehicle Repair Tasks folder is named Completion Time Analysis and this view compares the time that was estimated for the work and was recorded in the Total Work field with the actual time taken that the mechanics recorded on completion, in the Actual Work field on the Details tab of the task.

If management wishes to analyze the variance between the estimated time and the actual time taken for the jobs, it may benefit from the following view:

1. In the View Summary dialog box, click Fields, and select the fields Icon, Created, Owner, Subject, Notes, Date, Total Work, and Actual Work from the All Tasks field list, and Job No and Make Model from the User-defined fields in folder list, and click OK.

2. We will now create the following two new fields:

Name	Type	Format	Purpose
InTime	Yes/No	Icon	To toggle between a check meaning Yes and no check meaning No.
Total Actual Work	Number	All Digits	To bring down into this field the figure from the Total field from the previous record. The first entry for the first record will be zero as there will be no figure to bring down.

3. We will also create the following three formula fields:

Name	In the Formula Field window
Y/N	IIf([Actual Work]>[Total Work],"N",IIf([Actual Work]<=[Total Work],"Y"))
Diff	([Actual Work]-[Total Work])/60 & "hr(s)"
Total	([Actual Work]/60)+[Total Actual Work] & " hr(s)"

4. Continuing the design of the view, set Sort items by to Job No | Ascending.

5. From the Automatic Formatting option, click Add, and create the following rule:

Formatting Rule Name	Field	Condition	Value	Font Format	Purpose
Over Time	InTime	Equals	No	Red	Use red font for those items with no check in the InTime field

6. Exit the View Summary and from the Format Columns dialog box rename the following fields as follows:

Field name	New name	Format
Owner	Mechanic	
Created	Date	Day and date only (being the date the task was created)
Subject	Reg No	

7. Return to the View Summary and set Group by to Owner and stipulate not to show the field in the view.

What Just Happened?

We have created a view of completed tasks that fulfills two functions:

The first function will identify which tasks exceed the estimated time (Total Work) and will then calculate the difference between the estimated and actual times for the tasks.

The first function utilizes the following fields:

- The Y/N field where the formula says that if the actual time taken is greater than the estimated time, return the letter N, meaning No—the deadline was not met, or if the actual time taken is less than or equal to the estimated time, return the letter Y, meaning Yes—the deadline was met.

- The InTime field is only necessary to trigger the Automatic Formatting rule.

  Unfortunately, Automatic Formatting rules will not recognize Formula fields as Condition fields. So, having established from the Y/N field which tasks took more time than was estimated, we can emphasize these items with Red font by placing a check in the InTime field where there is N in the Y/N field and trigger the Automatic Formatting rule.

- The Diff field calculates the difference between the actual and the estimated times for the task.

The second function will produce a running sum of the time taken (Actual Work) over the period in view and for each Mechanic. This is achieved by the manual entry in the Total Actual Work field of the figure in the Total field of the previous item.

The Result

Here is the finished view:

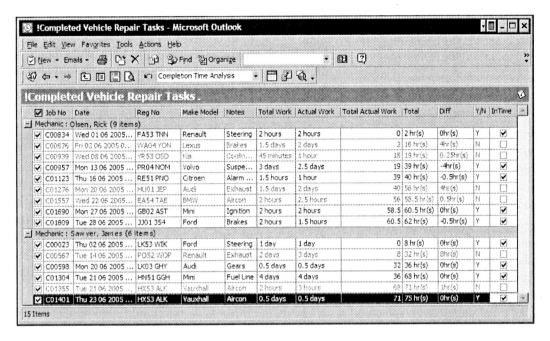

In Outlook, these calculations are made on the fly, so if you change the sort order of the records, the calculations will not adjust and recalculate. You would need to redo the manual entries in the Total Actual Work column.

For automatic and more complex calculations you would need to use another program such as Excel; and you can copy and paste these records into or export the entire folder to an Excel spreadsheet.

By selecting all the records in the folder and copying and pasting into an Excel spreadsheet, you will have an exact replica of the Outlook data, including the custom fields, but you will need to do some editing and reformatting before you will be able to manipulate the data.

	A	B	C	D	E	F	G	H	I	J	K
1	Job No	Date	Reg No	Make Mod	Notes	Total Work	Actual W	Total Ac	Total	Diff	Y/N
2	Mechanic Olsen, Rick										
3	C00834	Wed 01 06	FA53 TNN	Renault	Steering	2 hours	2 hours	0	2 hr(s)	0hr(s)	Y
4	C00876	Fri 03 06 2	WA04 YOI	Lexus	Brakes	1.5 days	2 days	2	18 hr(s)	4hr(s)	N
5	C00939	Wed 08 06	YR53 OSL	Kia	Cooling sy	45 minutes	1 hour	18	19 hr(s)	0.25hr(s)	N
6	C00957	Mon 13 06	PR04 NON	Volvo	Suspensio	3 days	2.5 days	19	39 hr(s)	-4hr(s)	Y
7	C01123	Thu 16 06	RE51 PNC	Citroen	Alarm & Lc	1.5 hours	1 hour	39	40 hr(s)	-0.5hr(s)	Y
8	C01276	Mon 20 06	HU01 JEP	Audi	Exhaust	1.5 days	2 days	40	56 hr(s)	4hr(s)	N
9	C01557	Wed 22 06	EA54 TAE	BMW	Aircon	2 hours	2.5 hours	56	58.5 hr(s)	0.5hr(s)	N
10	C01690	Mon 27 06	GB02 AST	Mini	Ignition	2 hours	2 hours	58.5	60.5 hr(s)	0hr(s)	Y
11	C01809	Tue 28 06	JJ01 354	Ford	Brakes	2 hours	1.5 hours	60.5	62 hr(s)	-0.5hr(s)	Y
12	Mechanic Sawyer, James										
13	C00023	Thu 02 06	LK53 WIK	Ford	Steering	1 day	1 day	0	8 hr(s)	0hr(s)	Y
14	C00567	Tue 14 06	PO52 WO	Renault	Exhaust	2 days	3 days	8	32 hr(s)	8hr(s)	N
15	C00598	Mon 20 06	LK03 GHY	Audi	Gears	0.5 days	0.5 days	32	36 hr(s)	0hr(s)	Y
16	C01304	Tue 21 06	HN51 GGF	Mini	Fuel Line	4 days	4 days	36	68 hr(s)	0hr(s)	Y
17	C01355	Tue 21 06	HX53 ALK	Vauxhall	Aircon	2 hours	3 hours	68	71 hr(s)	1hr(s)	N
18	C01401	Thu 23 06	HX53 ALK	Vauxhall	Aircon	0.5 days	0.5 days	71	75 hr(s)	0hr(s)	Y

Alternatively, if you export the folder to an Excel spreadsheet from the File | Import and Export, and follow the instructions, the custom fields you created will not be exported and the Outlook fields that you renamed will revert to the original Outlook names.

There will still be some editing and reformatting to do as all the fields in the Excel spreadsheet are formatted as General, including the StartDate field. You will notice that the time values in TotalWork and ActualWork have been exported to Excel in their raw format of minutes.

Completed Vehicle Repair Tasks.xls

	A	B	C	D	E	F
1	StartDate	Contacts	Subject	Notes	TotalWork	ActualWork
2	23 6 2005	Mrs Smith	HX53 ALK	Aircon	240	240
3	8 6 2005	Mrs Tolmuth	YR53 OSD	Cooling system	45	60
4	13 6 2005	Mrs Draper	PR04 NOM	Suspension	1440	1200
5	3 6 2005	Mrs Satin	WA04 YON	Brakes	720	960
6	1 6 2005	Miss Naisby	FA53 TNN	Steering	120	120
7	20 6 2005	Mrs Trapper	HU01 JEP	Exhaust	720	960
8	27 6 2005	Miss Jones	GB02 AST	Ignition	120	120
9	22 6 2005	Mr Belkin	EA54 TAE	Aircon	120	150
10	16 6 2005	Mr Colman	RE51 PNO	Alarm & Locking system	90	60
11	28 6 2005	Mr Edwards	JJ01 354	Brakes	120	90
12	14 6 2005	Mrs Klein	PO52 WOP	Exhaust	960	1440
13	21 6 2005	Mrs Smith	HX53 ALK	Aircon	120	180
14	2 6 2005	Miss Juniper	LK53 WIK	Steering	480	480
15	21 6 2005	Mr Brown	HN51 GGH	Fuel Line	1920	1920
16	20 6 2005	Miss Hopper	LK03 GHY	Gears	240	240
17						

\ Tasks /

In order for you to get the best benefit from the functionality of Outlook Tasks, many of your tasks need to reside in the default Tasks folder and the foregoing examples use Custom Views to control and make sense of the default Tasks folder.

We have also seen how even completed tasks have a value and we have extracted a lot of useful information from the completed tasks in our example.

There is one other type of task that we can manipulate creatively, and that is the unassigned task that does not require a reminder and therefore does not need to reside in the default Tasks folder.

Separate Tasks Folders

A separate Tasks folder can be just a To Do List and the tasks can be made to seem less overwhelming and more manageable when the tasks are grouped into categories that indicate their priority.

Outlook's priority grading of Low, Normal, and High is not always adequate so you may prefer to have a task grading system of Urgent, Today, This Week, and Sometime, or a numbering system that will order task priority by number, or a more explicit system that separates tasks into the actions required; for example, Email, Phone, Write, Visit, Delegate, or even a combination of all three.

A Tasks To Do List

1. Create a new Tasks folder named Tasks To Do List.

2. Create a new table type view from the Define Views | New option and name the view All To Do Tasks.

3. In the View Summary dialog box, click Fields, and select the fields: Complete, Subject, and Due Date, and click OK.

4. Create the following two new manual fields:

Name	Type	Format	Purpose
Category	Text	Text	To enter the name of the priority level e.g. 1-Urgent, 2-Today, 3-Tomorrow, 4-This week, 5-Next week, 6-Delegate, 7-Sometime
Type	Text	Text	To enter the type of action necessary e.g. email, phone, action, etc.

5. Set Group By to Category and stipulate not to show the field in the view.

6. From the Filter | Advanced tab create the following filter:

Field	Condition	Value
Complete	equals	no

7. From the Automatic Formatting option, click Add, and create the following formatting rule. The rules must be listed in this order to work properly.

Option	Name	Font	Condition
Rule 1	Urgent	Red	category contains 1
Rule 2	Today	Fuchsia	category contains 2
Rule 3	Task Text	Blue	category is empty

What Just Happened?

We created a Tasks folder to use as a personal To Do List. The items will not be updated and reminders are unnecessary so the list has been created as a separate folder outside of the default Tasks folder. It is a list that we can refer to in Outlook and/or print off and if we need to refer to the list regularly, it can remain open and minimized on screen.

To create a new Task, enter the details of the Task into the 'new item row' in the All To Do Tasks view and do not assign a category to the item. The new Task will create a new group called '(none)'. Just drag the new Task from the (none) group to one of the existing groupings e.g. 1-Urgent, 2-Today etc... and type a action for the Task into the Type field e.g. email, phone etc...

In this view, we want to group the tasks by their category, but if we use Outlook's Categories, we will not be able to drag a task from one category to another when it is, for example, downgrading from This week to Next week, without it being *added to* rather than *moved to* the second category. We would have to right-click the item and uncheck the unwanted category and then check the new category. By grouping on a field other than the Categories field, however, the field can be forced to change by dragging the item between the groups.

Completed tasks can be checked as complete and will disappear from the list, new tasks can be added and dragged to the appropriate category, and existing tasks can be promoted and demoted by being dragged through the priority category groups.

The new field, Type, indicates what the task entails; Email, Phone, Action, etc. and the Automatic Formatting rules color-code the priority levels for visual emphasis.

The Result

The unexpanded view of the folder:

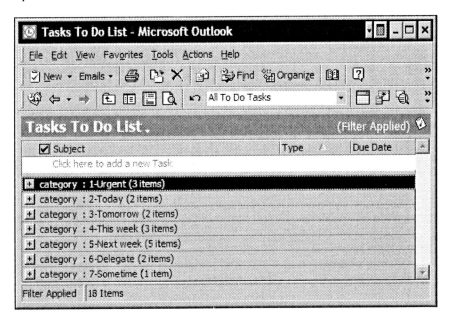

The expanded view:

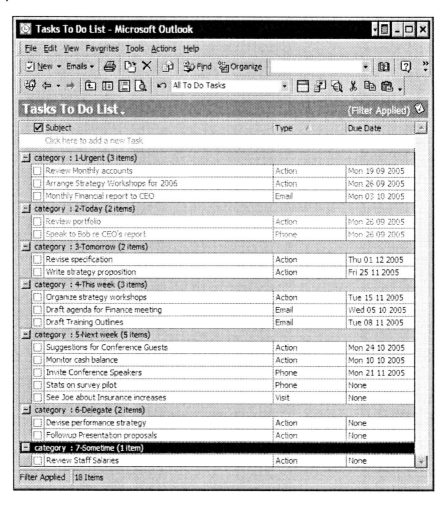

And a Print Preview of this task list with an appropriate header:

Reusable Tasks

Another use for separate Tasks folders would be for reusable tasks. If, for example there are processes, systems, or projects that you are often required to do that involve many steps or stages, you could have reusable tasks lists that act as checklists.

Meetings Checklist

For example, if you are a meetings secretary, you may wish to have a checklist to refer to, to ensure that you have remembered to do everything necessary for the meetings that you service. As you complete the items, check them as complete and when they have all been done and the meeting is over, remove the completion checks ready for the next meeting.

The example below groups the tasks by Categories and thereby places them into the timed stages for the meeting preparations. I have used the Outlook Categories field in this example because it is unlikely that you would need to move items between the categories. It is necessary to place a suffix in the Category name and before the subject text (e.g. A B C or 1 2 3) to ensure the correct order. A Due Date is optional.

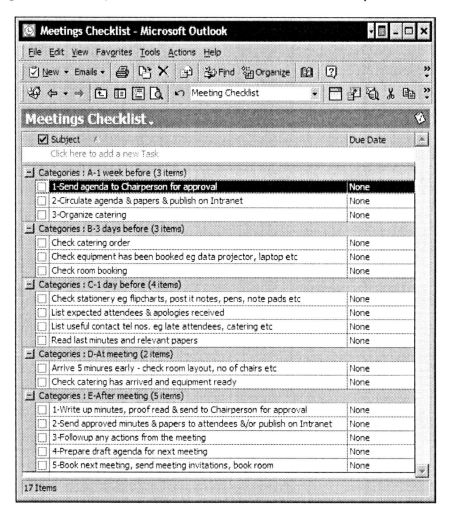

If you are responsible for several different meetings you may need a Meetings Checklist for each and you may have more than one checklist in progress at any one time. Once you have one Meetings Checklist Tasks folder set up, it is easy to copy it to create more and name the copied folders for the different meetings.

Induction Checklist

Another use for a reusable Tasks folder might be in the Human Resources department as a checklist for the process of staff induction.

The screenshot below shows a checklist for the induction of Bob Brown. There is a folder set up as the induction process template and this was copied and named specifically for Bob's induction. This particular checklist may not be reused, as it is a staff record and may need to be retained, but the template can be copied for new members of staff. A separate PST file could be created specifically to hold completed induction tasks lists for staff members, to avoid clogging the main PST file.

The standard By Category view has been used to view the progress of Bob's induction through the target categories, which represent the time stages, and the tasks themselves, representing the various steps in the induction of a new member of staff.

Where HR policy dictates, we could link certain of the induction items to Bob's contact record, for example, the items such as Induction complete and First performance review. This would begin a record of his progress within the company.

By including the Contacts field in this view, we can see which items have been linked and will be listed on the Activities tab of Bob's contact record.

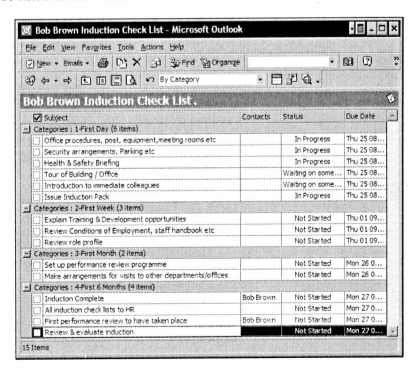

This is the Activities tab of Bob's contact record and the items will be updated to the Complete status when Bob has achieved these milestones.

Summary

Hopefully this chapter has encouraged you to think a little differently about Tasks.

Although tasks are synonymous with more work and jobs to do (as if you don't have enough to do already!), by being methodical and organized you can manage and control your tasks so that they work for you, saving you time and effort. Tasks even hold valuable information that can be exploited and reused. With a little imagination and creativity, Tasks can become a valuable and indispensable resource, transforming the way you work in Outlook.

Tasks have also introduced you to the final building block for the scenarios that are presented in the chapter that follows. Next we will bring together the Outlook tools and ideas that we have discussed so far to produce whole, interactive solutions that will transform Outlook into a **consummate information manager**.

4

Whole Solutions

So far we have explored unconventional uses of Outlook's individual components and we have utilized the business example of "Our Company" to demonstrate:

- Staff records: Recording and evaluating staff leave
- A vehicle pool: Recording and monitoring vehicle details, servicing, etc. and linking to users
- Suppliers: Organizing their records into an invaluable business directory
- Taxi booking records that could be applied to other services

In this way, we have been developing an Outlook solution for Our Company, but this solution is not quite complete, there is more that we can do for Our Company.

In this chapter, we will complete the solution for Our Company, integrating various Outlook and Office components, and will also explore another 'whole solution', a School-based example that we haven't yet introduced.

Our Company Solution

We will create a scenario involving both the Outlook and Office components.

Meeting Room Management

Meeting room bookings are commonly managed using a separate calendar, and these reservations may be for external organizations as well as for internal groups. The calendar in which these bookings are recorded will resemble an appointments calendar except that the items will refer to the rooms in which the meetings are being held rather than the meetings themselves. When more than one meeting is taking place in different rooms and at the same time, concurrent entries are inevitable and acceptable. A simplified and small portion of such a Meeting Rooms Calendar might look something like the following:

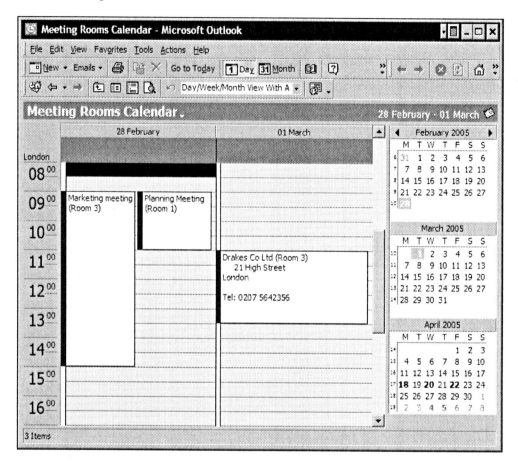

This view provides a clear image of what is happening in the meeting rooms over a short period of time. However, a schedule of meeting room activity over a greater period of time and with more detail about who booked the room, the revenue due from external bookings, etc. would be very useful for analysis and planning purposes.

Outlook can produce such a view of a Meeting Rooms Calendar that will

- Display a schedule of all current and future room booking details
- Distinguish between internal and external reservations
- Automatically calculate the cost to the external hirer

Before we begin to design this view of the Meeting Rooms Calendar, there should be in place Contacts records for hirers of the rooms, whether they are colleagues in the same company or customers in external organizations. We also need Contacts records for each of the meeting rooms and a Contacts folder named Meeting Rooms in which to store them. Although Outlook Contacts folders are normally associated with storing the details of people, there is no reason why Contacts folders cannot hold the records of inanimate objects. By creating and manipulating Contacts records for items, Outlook truly becomes a supreme information manager.

Before building the set of meeting room contacts, we first need to create the new Contacts folder. This is done in the usual way by right-clicking in the Outlook folder list and choosing New Folder and naming the folder Meeting Rooms.

Creating Contacts records for hirers needs no special instruction and the only field that needs to be completed on the Contact form for the rooms is the Full Name field; the details of the rooms will be recorded in the view and not in the Contact record.

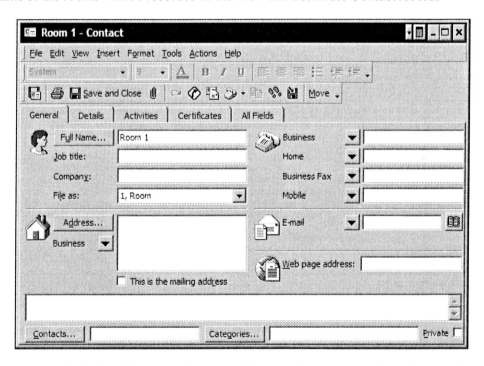

We now have individual Contacts for each of the meeting rooms and Contacts for the hirers, all of which we can link to the bookings in the Meeting Rooms Calendar. We can now create the view of the Meeting Rooms Contacts folder that will display the details of the rooms.

Creating a Meeting Rooms View

1. Create a new table-type view from the Define Views | New option and name the view Meeting Rooms.

2. In the View Summary dialog box, click Fields and select the field Full Name, and click OK.

3. We will create the following manual fields:

Name	Type	Format	Purpose
Capacity	Number	Raw	To enter the number of people the room can accommodate
Rate per hr	Currency	2 decimal places	To record the cost per hour to hire each room
Facilities	Text	Text	To enter the equipment etc. available in each room

4. Rename the Full Name field to Meeting Room, from the Format Columns dialog box.

All four fields require you to enter manually the details about the rooms i.e. the name or number of the room, how many people it can accommodate, the facilities that it has e.g. projector, flip charts, whiteboard, teleconference facilities, etc., and the hourly rate for external hire.

The Result

The following screenshot shows Meeting Rooms view:

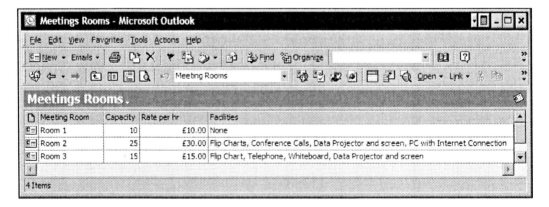

Creating the Meeting Room Calendar View

The steps to create this view begin with linking the bookings to the Contacts forms of the internal or external hirers and to the Contacts forms of the rooms. This will provide a bookings history by room and by person or company.

This view can also be adapted to display reservations by room, by date, by occupant, or by internal or external booking just by changing the way that the items are grouped. Finally, we will see how the calendar appointment form can be redesigned to integrate with Microsoft Word to print an invoice for the room hire and how Outlook can produce a monthly statement for the hirer.

1. Create two new Categories for the room bookings named Internal and External.

2. Enter room bookings into the Calendar in the normal Day/Week/Month view and assign either the Internal or External category depending on whether it is an internal or external hirer.

3. Create a new table-type view from the Define Views | New option and name the view Meeting room calendar.

4. In the View Summary dialog box, click Fields, and select the fields: Location, Subject, Contacts, Start, End, and Duration, and click OK.

5. We will create three new manual fields that will be used to build one Address field and these fields will also be used later in the development of the form and the printing of the invoice:

Name	Type	Format	Purpose
Add Line 1	Text	Text	To enter the first address line of the hirer
Add Line 2	Text	Text	To enter the second address line of the hirer
Add Line 3	Text	Text	To enter the third address line of the hirer

Name	Type	In the Formula Field window
Start Time	Formula	Format([Start],"h:mm")
Room Chrge	Formula	IIf([Location]="Room 1",Format(10,"Currency"),IIf([Location]="Room 2",Format(30,"Currency"),IIf([Location]="Room 3",Format(15,"Currency"),"Rate?")))
Total Fee	Formula	IIf([Categories]="External",Format([Room Chrge]*[Duration]/60,"Currency"),IIf([Categories]="Internal","Internal"))
Address	Combination	[Add Line 1] [Add Line 2] [Add Line 3]

6. To restrict the bookings in the view to current and future, add a filtering criterion. From the Filter | Advanced tab create the following filter:

Field	Condition	Value
Start	On or after	today

7. To distinguish internal from external room bookings, apply the following Automatic Formatting rule:

Formatting Rule Name	Field	Condition	Value	Font Format
Internal	Categories	Is(exactly)	Internal	Blue

8. Exit the View Summary and from the Format Columns dialog box modify the following fields as shown:

Field name	New name	Format
Subject	Booking For:	
Start	Date	Date only
End	End	Time only

What Just Happened?

We have created the basic view as described and the fields will operate as follows:

- The Start Time field repeats the Start field but formats the contents to show only the hours and minutes, ("h:mm"). Outlook does not allow you to place a field in the header area more than once but you achieve this by placing the field that you wish to repeat within a custom field.

- The Room Chrge field will automatically return the room fee depending on the room number entered in the Location field. The Format function ensures that the result is formatted as currency; so £10.00 for Room 1, £30.00 for Room 2 and £15.00 for Room 3. If no room number is entered in the Location field, this field will return "Rate?", indicating that a rate cannot be determined unless a room number is entered.

- The formula in the Total Fee field is dependent upon the creation of the two new categories, Internal and External, and meeting room bookings in the calendar being assigned accordingly. The formula says that if the item is an external room booking (i.e. the calendar item has been assigned the External category) the charge should be calculated as the Room Chrge multiplied by the Duration, divided by 60. It is necessary to divide the Duration by 60 because the Duration field actually holds time values in minutes even though it may display in hours. This part of the calculation is enclosed with the Format(.............."Currency") function so that the result will be in currency format. If the calendar item is assigned to the Internal category the field returns the word Internal. This assumes that no charges are levied for internal bookings.

- The three manual address line fields have been concatenated into the single Address field to save space in the view and can be removed from the view by dragging them off the field header bar. However, three separate address line fields are required so that they can appear on separate lines in the merge to the Word invoice template described later.

The Result

With all the fields in place, you can enter bookings into the Meeting Rooms Calendar in the usual Day/Week/Month view and then switch to the Meeting room calendar view to obtain a condensed view of all current and future meeting room bookings. The external reservations have the charge already calculated and the internal bookings are in blue font with no charge.

Location	Booking For:	Address	Contacts	Date	Start time	End	Duration	Room Chrge	Total fee
Room 1	XYZ & Co	229 Walles Lane Liverpool L...	Room 1; XYZ & Co	Tue 30 08 2005	9:30	14:30	5 hours	£10.00	£50.00
Room 2	Postlethwaite & Sons	167 Romano Street Birmingh...	Room 2; Postlethwaite ...	Tue 30 08 2005	9:00	11:30	2.5 hours	£30.00	£75.00
Room 3	Underwood Machinery Ltd	67 Tripod Way London EC1...	Room 3; Underwood M...	Thu 25 08 2005	15:00	17:00	2 hours	£15.00	£30.00
Room 1	Underwood Machinery Ltd	67 Tripod Way London EC1...	Room 1; Underwood M...	Wed 24 08 2005	14:00	17:00	3 hours	£10.00	£30.00
Room 3	Dodgey Dongles	87 New Brighton Street Liver...	Room 3; Dodgey Dongles	Tue 23 08 2005	11:00	13:30	2.5 hours	£15.00	£37.50
Room 1	Strategy Meeting	Finance Dept	Room 1; Anne Dodsworth	Tue 16 08 2005	15:30	16:00	30 minutes	£10.00	Internal
Room 1	Drakes Co Ltd	21 High Street London EC10...	Room 1; Drakes Co Ltd	Tue 16 08 2005	13:30	14:00	30 minutes	£10.00	£5.00
Room 3	Drakes Co Ltd	21 High Street London EC10...	Room 1; Drakes Co Ltd	Tue 16 08 2005	13:30	14:00	30 minutes	£15.00	£7.50
Room 2	Dodgey Dongles	15 West Street Manchester ...	Room 3; Dodgey Dongles	Wed 08 06 2005	15:30	17:00	1.5 hours	£30.00	£45.00
Room 1	GBF Project Board Mtg	Sales Dept	Room 1; Paula Wilson	Mon 16 05 2005	14:00	16:00	2 hours	£10.00	Internal
Room 3	Drakes Co Ltd	21 High Street London EC10...	Room 3; Drakes Co Ltd	Thu 05 05 2005	12:00	14:00	2 hours	£15.00	£30.00
Room 1	HR Meeting	HR	Room 1; Laura Callahan	Wed 04 05 2005	8:00	14:30	6.5 hours	£10.00	Internal
Room 1	Drakes Co Ltd	21 High Street London EC10...	Room 1; Drakes Co Ltd	Fri 22 04 2005	8:00	14:30	6.5 hours	£10.00	£65.00
Room 3	Dodgey Dongles	15 West Street Manchester ...	Room 3; Dodgey Dongles	Wed 20 04 2005	10:00	12:00	2 hours	£15.00	£30.00
Room 3	Drakes Co Ltd	21 High Street London EC10...	Room 3; Drakes Co Ltd	Mon 18 04 2005	11:30	14:00	2.5 hours	£15.00	£37.50
Room 3	Drakes Co Ltd	21 High Street London EC10...	Room 3; Drakes Co Ltd	Tue 01 03 2005	11:00	13:30	2.5 hours	£15.00	£37.50
Room 3	Marketing meeting	Sales Dept	Room 3; Laura Callahan	Mon 28 02 2005	9:00	15:00	6 hours	£15.00	Internal
Room 1	Planning Meeting	Management	Room 1; Victoria Ashw...	Mon 28 02 2005	9:00	11:00	2 hours	£10.00	Internal

Filter Applied   24 Items

This view does not group the bookings in any way, but other views can be created based upon this view that show the bookings grouped in various ways, or grouping can be achieved by dragging the appropriate field to the Group By area. Useful booking schedules can then be printed.

The following screenshots display groupings with respect to Location, Booking For, Date, and Categories respectively:

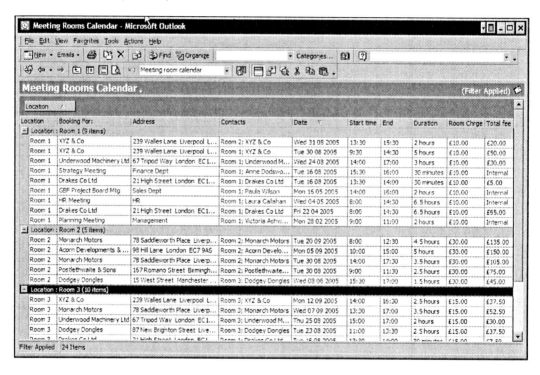

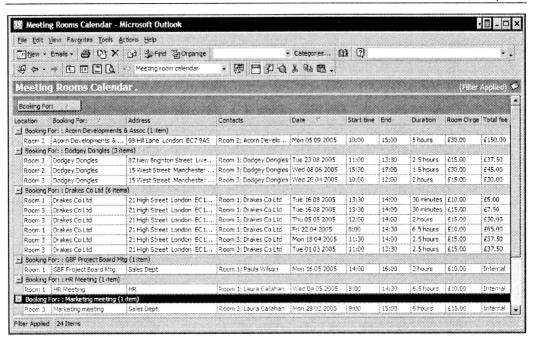

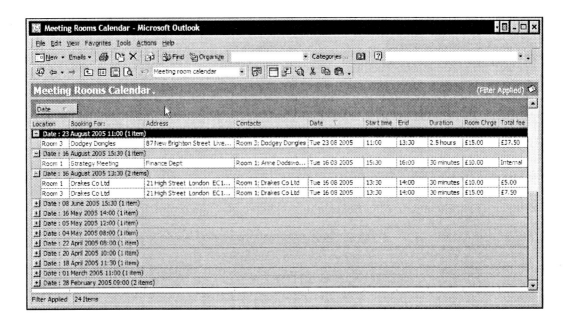

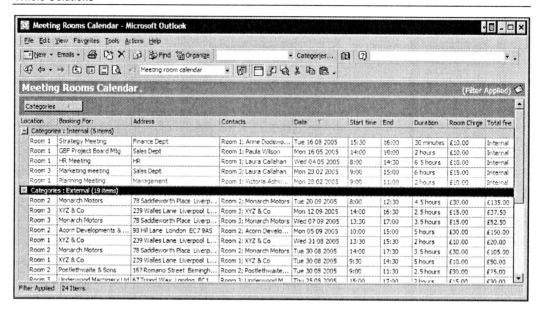

Invoicing Meeting Room Bookings

We are now going to add a page to the appointments form (meeting room booking) in the Meeting Rooms Calendar folder. The added page will contain extra details of the room booking and a print button that will run code to activate an invoice template. Fields from the Outlook calendar item will merge with the Word invoice template to produce an invoice for the room hire. The invoice can then be saved and printed.

To produce the Word template, we will require a basic template for an invoice and the insertion in the appropriate places of a Word text form field for each of the Outlook fields.

Text form fields are inserted into a Word document by clicking the Text Form Field button on the Forms toolbar in Word. By right-clicking on each inserted text form field and choosing Properties you can make a note of the Bookmark name (Text1, Text2, etc.) of each field for use in the following code and set the formatting of the data that will appear in the field. The formatting for the fields in this example is detailed further on in this text.

Once we have added the extra page to the meeting room booking form, the form will have an extra tab named Print and the Print page of the Appointment Form will look something like the screenshot shown opposite.

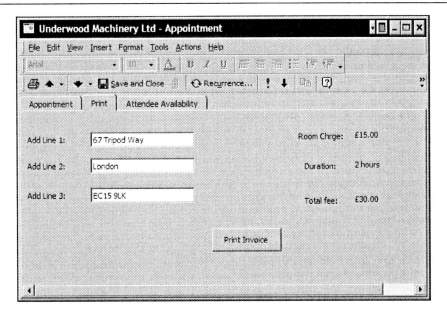

Creating the Appointment Form

1. Open a new appointment form in the Meeting Rooms Calendar folder and access design mode from Tools | Forms | Design This Form.

2. Click the tab (P.2) and first make it visible from Form | Display This Page, then rename it Print from Form | Rename Page.

3. From the Field Chooser dialog box, drag the Duration field onto the form and, under User-defined fields in folder, drag and place on the form the five fields we created, Room Chrge, Total Fee, Add Line 1, Add Line 2, and Add Line 3.

4. Create the following new field:

Name	In the Formula Field window
Meeting Duration	[Duration]/60

Do not drag this field on to the form. We are using the Outlook Duration field on the form because it will display the time span in hours. We cannot use the Outlook Duration field for the Word template because it will revert to its underlying format of minutes. The Meeting Duration field we have just created will remain as a 'user-defined field in this folder' and will be picked up by the following code and used in the 8th bookmark. This field will be used just for the merge into the Word template and will ensure that the duration of the meeting will be shown as hours in the final invoice.

5. From the Control Toolbox drag a Command Button onto the form.

6. Right-click on the CommandButton and change the caption to read Print Invoice.

7. To add the print code behind the CommandButton, click the View Code button on the Form Design toolbar, 🖵 and add the following code in the Script Editor:

```
Sub cmdPrint_Click()
    Set oWordApp = CreateObject("Word.Application")
    If oWordApp Is Nothing Then
        MsgBox "Couldn't start word."
    Else
        Dim oWordApp
        Dim oWordDoc
        Dim bolPrintBackground

        ' Open new document
        Set oDoc = oWordApp.Documents.Add("C:\Documents and
Settings\UserName\Application Data\Microsoft\Templates\Room Hire
Invoice.dot")

        ' Set 1st bookmark to contact's Name
        oDoc.FormFields("Text1").Result = CStr(Item.Subject)

        ' Set 2nd bookmark to Address Line 1
        strMyField = Item.UserProperties.Find("Add Line 1")
        oDoc.FormFields("Text2").Result = strMyField

        ' Set 3rd bookmark to Address Line 2
        strMyField1 = Item.UserProperties.Find("Add Line 2")
        oDoc.FormFields("Text3").Result = strMyField1

        ' Set 4th bookmark to Address Line 3
        strMyField2 = Item.UserProperties.Find("Add Line 3")
        oDoc.FormFields("Text4").Result = strMyField2

        ' Set 5th bookmark to the Room
        oDoc.FormFields("Text5").Result = CStr(Item.Location)

        ' Set 6th bookmark to the booking's start date & time
        oDoc.FormFields("Text6").Result = CStr(Item.Start)

        ' Set 7th bookmark to the booking's end date & time
        oDoc.FormFields("Text7").Result = CStr(Item.End)

        ' Set 8th bookmark to the booking duration
        strMyField3 = Item.UserProperties.Find("Meeting Duration")
        oDoc.FormFields("Text8").Result = strMyField3

        ' Set 9th bookmark to the Room Rate per hour
        strMyField4 = Item.UserProperties.Find("Room Chrge")
        oDoc.FormFields("Text9").Result = strMyField4

        ' Set 10th bookmark to the Total Charge
```

```
        strMyField5 = Item.UserProperties.Find("Total fee")
        oDoc.FormFields("Text10").Result = strMyField5

    ' Set 11th bookmark to the Amount Due
        strMyField5 = Item.UserProperties.Find("Total fee")
        oDoc.FormFields("Text11").Result = strMyField5

    ' Set 12th bookmark to the Invoice Date
        oDoc.FormFields("Text12").Result = CStr(Item.End)


    oWordApp.Visible=True


        Set oDoc = Nothing
        Set oWordApp = Nothing
    End If
End Sub
```

8. Close the Script Editor, open the Tools menu in the form, still in Design mode, and select Forms | Publish Form As and name and publish the form to the Meeting Rooms Calendar folder.

9. In the General tab of the Properties of the Meeting Rooms Calendar folder, open the When posting to this folder, use: drop-down box, and select the Meeting Room form. This will tell Outlook to use this form when creating new items in this folder.

10. You will need to alter the tenth line of the previous code to the path of the Word invoice template on your system and print the invoice on company headed paper.

What Just Happened?

The shaded fields in the Word template are all the Form Text Fields that were inserted into the invoice template and these have been assigned the Word bookmark names e.g. Text1 etc. The code behind the Outlook form is locating those bookmarks, e.g. oDoc.FormFields("Text1") and is inserting the Outlook fields e.g. CStr(Item.Subject).

For the custom, user-defined fields the following syntax is used to find those fields and to transfer the field contents (e.g. Add Line 1) to the Word bookmarks (e.g. Text2) on the form:

```
strMyField = Item.UserProperties.Find("Add Line 1")
oDoc.FormFields("Text2").Result = strMyField
```

You will notice that the End Date field [CStr(Item.End)] has been used twice in the code, first as the date of the invoice (formatted as date only) and secondly as the end date for the room booking (formatted as date and time).

The remaining formats of the Word text form's fields are as follows:

Word Text Form Field	Type	Format
Add Line fields	Regular text	No special formatting; text will appear as entered
Room Number	Number	**Number format:** `0`
Start and End fields	Date	**Date format:** `dd/MM/yyyy HH:mm`
Duration	Number	**Number format:** `0.00 hrs` The standard number format 0.00 is used with the hrs suffix.
Room Rate per hour, Charge & Amount Due	Number	**Number format:** `£#,##0.00;(£#,##0.00)`

The Result

The Word form template that we have created when printed on the letter headed paper of our fictitious company "Our Company Ltd." would produce the invoice as shown below:

Our Company Ltd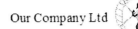

Invoice

TO: Underwood Machinery Ltd Text1
          67 Tripod Way   Text2
          London Text3
          EC15 9LK Text4

DATE: 25 August 2005 Text12

RE: Room Hire

Meeting Room No: 3 Text5

Start Date & Time:	End Date & Time:	Duration:	Room Rate Per hour:	Charge:
25/08/2005 15:00	25/08/2005 17:00	2.00 hrs	£15.00	£30.00
Text6	Text7	Text8	Text9	Text10

Amount Due = £30.00
Text11

Signed
For & on Behalf of
Our Company

Meeting Room Maintenance

We can also include in this solution the means to track the repair and updating of meeting room facilities by creating Tasks for maintenance items.

For example, a task can be created for an air conditioning fault that is reported for meeting Room 1.

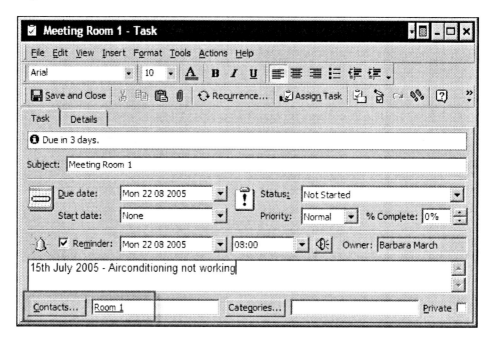

To enable updating by the maintenance crew, the task is created in the default Tasks folder and it is also linked via the Contacts button to Room 1 in the Meeting Rooms Contacts folder.

The Meeting Rooms Contacts folder is linked to the default Tasks folder so that the Activities tab of the Room 1 contact record will display a history of maintenance items for that room.

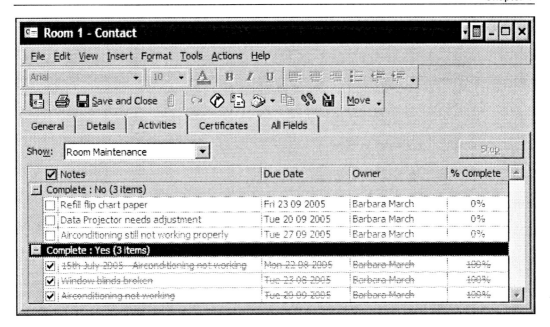

We can now monitor, for example, how many times the air conditioning in Room 1 has been repaired and the Owner field will tell us who is responsible for this. We can track the progress of maintenance items and determine if the room is ready to be used.

Using the Meeting Room Solution

Open a new form in the Meeting Rooms Calendar. This will be a blank, custom, meeting room form that we created specifically for the Meeting room calendar. Complete the fields on the Appointment page, and on the Print page of the form, if it is an external booking, manually enter the postal address of the client in the Add Line fields 1, 2 and 3. If it is an internal booking, complete just the first address line with the name of the department in your company that is booking the room. Outlook will pick up the dates from the dates of the booking, will calculate the cost of the room hire, and display the details in the corresponding fields on the Print page.

For all this to work properly, it is important that you remember to:

1. Assign either the Internal or External category

2. Link the booking to the relevant room in the Meetings Rooms' Contacts folder and the contacts record of either the company that is hiring the room (external booking) or, for an internal booking, the relevant person in your company

By linking the room booking to the external client company or to the internal staff member, double-clicking on the link within the calendar item will give you access to the details of the hirer should you need to contact them about the booking.

You will be able to view the full bookings record and income history for individual rooms from the Activities tab of the room contact record:

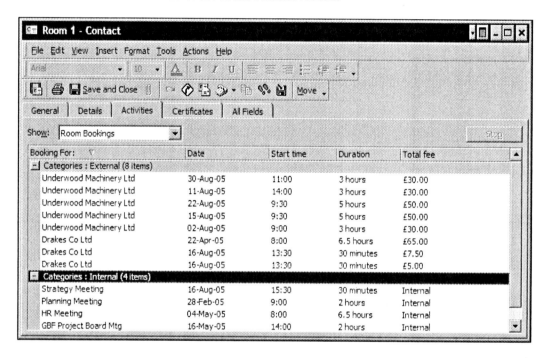

The following screenshot shows the external bookings history of the hirer:

The following screenshot shows the internal bookings history of the hirer:

Invoicing Room Bookings

To invoice an external room booking, open the booking appointment in the Meetings Rooms Calendar, click the Print tab and click the Print Invoice button. All the details of the booking will be transferred to the Word invoice template and the invoice document will open with all the fields complete. You are then able to print and save the invoice like any other Word document.

Unfortunately, Outlook does not allow you to print a list or schedule of the items appearing on the Activities tab of a contacts record to create a statement to present to clients.

However, you can create individual views of the Meetings Rooms' Calendar folder that will filter by client and by current month, to produce a statement of room bookings per client.

For example the Underwood Machinery company has made several meeting room bookings as the Activities tab of its contact record shows in the screenshot overleaf and they will have been invoiced for each separate booking.

If, at the end of August, we wanted to send the client a statement of all the bookings and invoices for August we would need to create the following view of the Meeting room calendar that filtered meetings for the Underwood Machinery company in August.

Creating the Calendar View for Bookings and Invoices

1. From the Define Views | Copy option, copy the Meeting room calendar view and name the copy view (in this instance) Underwood Mach Statement.

2. From the Filter | Appointments and Meetings tab create the first filter:

Search for the word(s)	in
Underwood	subject field only

3. From the Filter | Advanced tab create the second filter:

Field	Condition	Value
Start	Between	1/8/05 and 31/8/05

4. Set up the Print Preview of this view with a suitable header and print the statement on company headed paper:

What Just Happened?

We have worked through a way of using Outlook to manage meeting rooms and their bookings. This method could be applied to other forms of room hire, for example, booking rooms in a small hotel or guesthouse; the rate would be per day and not per hour and there would be other charges to be included, but the principle would be the same.

The Result

The following is the Print Preview of the Statement of Bookings done in the month of August 2005:

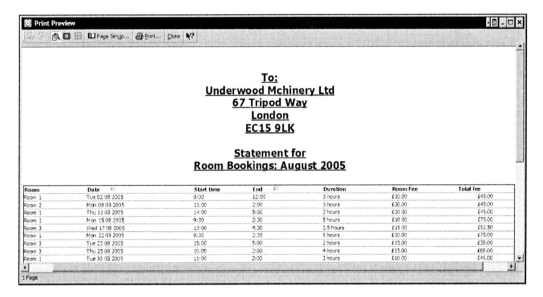

Sales

We can also create a method of managing email orders for Our Company that will automatically group and sort the orders and provide a quick and easy start to the order process.

Our Company manufactures various types of nuts: Topnuts, Hipnuts, Bobnuts, and Dropnuts and the company has instructed its customers to send orders for the various types of nuts by email, stipulating that the email orders must mention the word Order in the subject line and then the variety of nuts being ordered, e.g. Order: Topnut. The body of the email can then go into greater detail about the order including the number of items required. The emails are sent to the Order Clerk at Our Company.

The company has a team of salespeople who are responsible for specific customers and they earn commission and bonuses annually on the total values of the orders placed.

The email orders are received in the Order Clerk's Inbox and he/she has created a mail folder specifically for email orders and a custom view of the folder that presents the orders as shown in the next image:

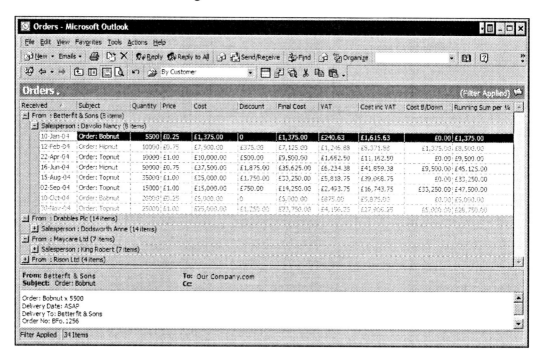

Before constructing this folder and view, the following should be created:

1. Categories for each salesperson (the category being the name of the salesperson).

2. InBox rules for the incoming email orders for each customer. The rules will move emails from specified customers that have Order in the subject line to the Orders folder. The rules will also forward the emails to the appropriate account salesperson and assign the emails to the salesperson's category. For example:

Apply this rule after the message arrives:

From Betterfit & Sons
and with Order in the subject
Assign it to the Davolio Nancy category
and forward it to Davolio Nancy
and move it to the Orders folder

Creating the Orders Mail Folder

1. Create a new Mail folder named Orders.

2. Create a new table-type view from the Define Views | New option and name the view By Customer.

3. In the View Summary dialog box, click Fields, and select the fields: Received, Subject, and Categories, and click OK.

4. We now create the following two new manual fields:

Name	Type	Format	Purpose
Quantity	Number	Raw	To enter manually the quantity of nuts being ordered
Cost B/Down	Currency	2 digits	To bring down manually the previous Final Cost value to create a running sum

5. And the following five formula fields:

Name	In the Formula Field window
Price	Format(IIf([Subject]="Order: Bobnut",0.25,IIf([Subject]="Order: Dropnut",0.6,IIf([Subject]="Order: Hipnut",0.75,IIf([Subject]="Order: Topnut",1," ")))),"currency")
Cost	Format(([Price]*[Quantity]),"currency")
Discount	IIf([Cost]>5000,Format(([Cost]*0.05),"currency"),"0")
Final Cost	Format([Cost]-[Discount],"currency")
VAT	Format(([Final Cost]*0.175),"currency")
Cost inc VAT	Format([Final Cost]*1.175,"currency")
Running Sum per ¼	Format([Cost B/Down]+[Final Cost],"currency")

6. Set Group By to From, Then by to Categories.

7. Set Sort items by to Received.

8. In Other Settings activate Show Preview Pane (Preview all items in Outlook 2003).

9. From the Filter | Advanced tab create the following filter:

Field	Condition	Value
Received	Between	1/1/04 and 31/12/04

Separate views can be created to filter different time spans, e.g. the current year for daily active use or, as in this case, a previous year to view a full year's sales.

10. From the Automatic Formatting option click Add and create the following formatting rules:

Formatting Rule Name	Field	Condition	Value	Font Format
1st ¼	Received	Between	1/1/04 and 31/3/04	Green
2nd ¼	Received	Between	1/4/04 and 30/6/04	Blue
3rd ¼	Received	Between	1/7/04 and 30/9/04	Purple
4th ¼	Received	Between	1/10/04 and 31/12/04	Olive

11. Exit the View Summary and from the Format Columns dialog box rename the following field as shown:

Field name	New name
Categories	Salesperson

12. Remove from the view the fields From and Salesperson (Categories) by dragging them from the field header area.

13. Create a link between the Contacts folder that contains the customers' contacts records to the Orders mail folder.

14. Create a Contacts folder each year of sales, for example in this case Sales 2004.

15. Create or copy the contacts records for the salespeople into these folders.

16. Create a new view for these Contacts folders that can be used on all Contacts folder, from the Define Views | New option and name the view Sales and Commission.

17. In the View Summary dialog box, click Fields, and select the field: File As and click OK.

18. We will now create four new manual fields as follows:

Name	Type	Format	Purpose
2004 1st ¼	Currency	2 digits	To enter manually the sales figures for the first quarter
2004 2nd ¼	Currency	2 digits	To enter manually the sales figures for the second quarter
2004 3rd ¼	Currency	2 digits	To enter manually the sales figures for the third quarter
2004 4th ¼	Currency	2 digits	To enter manually the sales figures for the fourth quarter

19. And the following three formula fields:

Name	In the Formula Field window
Total Sales	[2004 1st ¼]+[2004 2nd ¼]+[2004 3rd ¼]+[2004 4th ¼]
Commission	Format([Total Sales]*0.01,"Currency")
Bonus	IIf([Total Sales]>300000,"£5,000.00","")

What Just Happened?

We have created a solution for managing email orders that firstly forwards a copy of the order request to the relevant salesperson and secondly moves the email to an Orders folder. The Outlook incoming mail rules and the setup of the view of the Orders folder ensure that the emails are grouped first by the customer and then by the salesperson in this folder and the email orders are colored differently according to the quarter of the year in which they are received.

The Orders Clerk obtains the quantity being ordered from the preview pane of the emails, and enters that figure into the Quantity field.

The formula fields operate as follows:

1. The Price field tests the Subject field of the email and returns the item price according to the item ordered.

2. The Cost field multiplies Cost and Quantity to return the net value of the order.

3. The Discount field calculates a discount of 5% only when the Cost field exceeds £5000 and defaults to zero.

4. The Final Cost field subtracts Discount from Cost.N

5. The VAT field calculates the VAT @ 17.5%.

6. The Total Cost field adds Final Cost and VAT.

7. The Running Sum per ¼ is calculated when the Running Sum per ¼ figure is brought down to the next line.

The Result

Here is the finished view of the Orders mail folder:

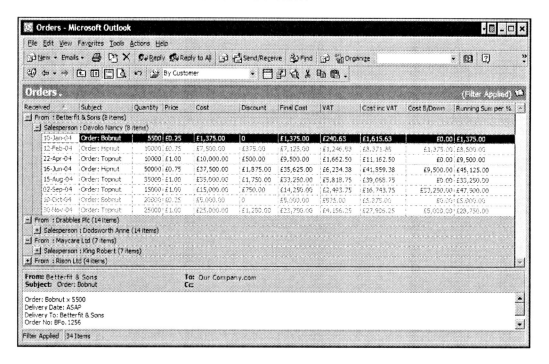

The linking of this folder with the customers Contacts folder enables the Orders Clerk to view the orders on the Activities tab of the individual customers' contact records as shown:

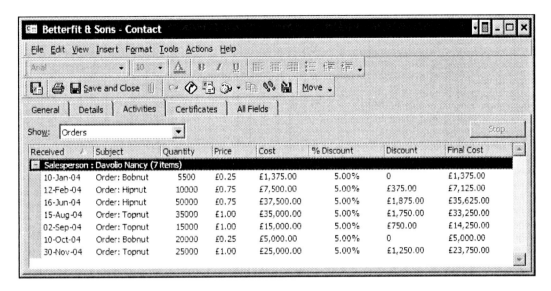

Creating the Contacts folder, Sales 2004, enables the calculation and recording of sales commission per salesperson. The figures for the fields 2004 1st ¼ to 2004 4th ¼ are taken from the Running Sum per ¼ field in the Orders mail folder.

Transcribing these figures from one set of fields to another is made easier by the color-coding of the different quarters of the year and with the Orders folder open in the background and the Sales 2004 folder open in a new window in the foreground as shown in the screenshot overleaf:

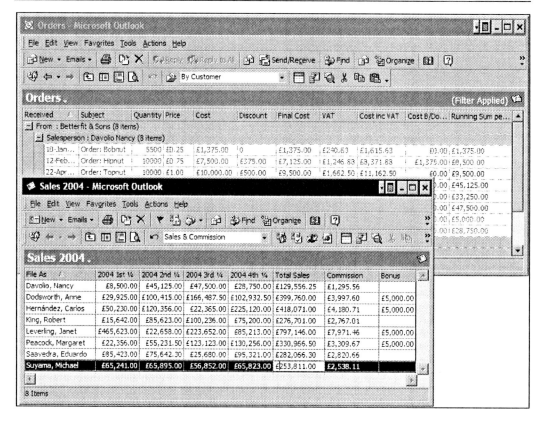

The Total Sales field is adding all the sales from the four quarters, the Commission field is calculating a commission for the sales team of 1% of Total Sales and the Bonus is calculated where sales exceed £300,000.

That completes the solution for Our Company and, although it may not fit your company, we are sure that the examples will generate ideas that will produce beneficial solutions.

The next scenario introduces Our School.

Our School Solution

We are now going to create another scenario in Outlook that will incorporate and link more of its components. The Our School Solution will contain separate Contacts folders for students, study subjects, teachers, and classrooms. There will be a separate Calendar for the classes in each subject, a Tasks folder for distributing assignments and monitoring their progress, a Journal folder containing student progress reports and a Notes folder for recording detentions etc.

These items will be linked to the students' contact records so that the Activities tab will show the classes they have attended, their detention record, the progress of their assignments and will have a direct link to their progress reports.

We shall begin by creating four separate Contacts folders.

Creating the Students Contacts Folders

1. Begin by creating new categories for each student class, e.g. 3a, 3b, etc.

2. Then create a new Contacts folder named Students and a new subfolder with the title of the name of the first class, for example, 3a. Once we have set up the definition of this folder, we shall copy the folder for the remaining classes.

3. Create a new table-type view from the Define Views | New option and name the view Students.

4. In the View Summary dialog box, click Fields and select the fields: Full Name, Contacts, Language, Mobile Phone, Home Address, Spouse, Home Phone, and click OK.

5. We will now create the following three new manual fields:

Name	Type	Format	Purpose
M/F	Text	Text	To enter M or F to indicate gender
DoB	Date	Date only	To enter a date of birth
Allergies	Text	Text	To record the student's allergies

6. We will also add the following Combination field:

Name	In the Combination Field window
Next of Kin	[Spouse] ~ [Home Phone]

7. And the following four formula fields:

Name	In the Formula Field window	To be Shown in the View
Age Months	DateDiff("m",[DoB],Date())	NO
Age yrs	Int([Age Months]/12)	NO

Name	In the Formula Field window	To be Shown in the View
Age M Diff	[Age Months]-([Age yrs]*12)	NO
Age	[Age yrs] & " yr(s) " & [Age M Diff] & " mnth(s)"	YES

8. Exit the View Summary and from the Format Columns dialog box rename the following field as shown:

Field name	New name
Contacts	Subjects

9. Once you are happy with the fields and the formatting of the folder, copy the class folder into the main Students folder as many times as there are classes and rename the copies to the class names, for example, in our case, we have classes 3a, 3b, 4a, 4b, 5a, 5b, 6a, and 6b.

10. Enter student data into the appropriate class folders by completing a new contact records for each student in that class. Initially complete the Full Name, Home Address, Home Phone, Mobile Phone fields on the General tab, and the Spouse field on the Details tab of the Contacts form. Also apply the relevant class category to each student record.

11. Save the Contacts record and in the Students view, complete the manual fields—M/F, DoB, Language, and Allergies.

What Just Happened?

We have created folders that will hold student information in their classes. As they move upwards, en bloc, through the school we can change the names of folders, create new folders, and delete the folders of student classes that have left the school.

In the Students view of each class folder, the Age field will automatically calculate and other fields will be automatically populated by the information entered. The one field that remains empty at this stage is the Contacts field (renamed Subjects). This field will remain blank until each student record is linked to the subjects they are studying and we shall do this once we have set up a Contacts folder for the study subjects.

The Result

Once the student records have been linked to their subjects, and data has been entered, the class folders will look like this:

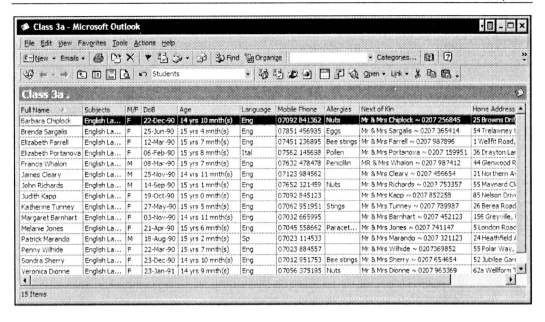

Creating the Subjects Contacts Folder

1. Begin by creating new categories for each study subject e.g. English Language, Mathematics, History, etc.

2. Then create a new Contacts folder named @Subjects.

3. Create a new table-type view from the Define Views | New option and name the view Subjects.

4. In the View Summary dialog box, click Fields and select the fields: Full Name and Contacts, and click OK.

5. We will now create the following new manual field:

Name	Type	Format	Purpose
Teacher	Text	Text	To enter the name of the teacher for each subject

6. Exit the View Summary and from the Format Columns dialog box rename the following fields as shown:

Field name	New name
Full Name	Subjects
Contacts	Students

What Just Happened?

We have created a folder in which to list the study subjects and the relevant teachers' names. We can now go back to the individual student records in the class folders created above, and link the subjects to the student records from the Contacts button on the student Contacts form.

The Result

The subjects will show in the Students view of the class folders under Subjects and the students will show in the @Subjects folder under Students, as can be seen in the following screenshot:

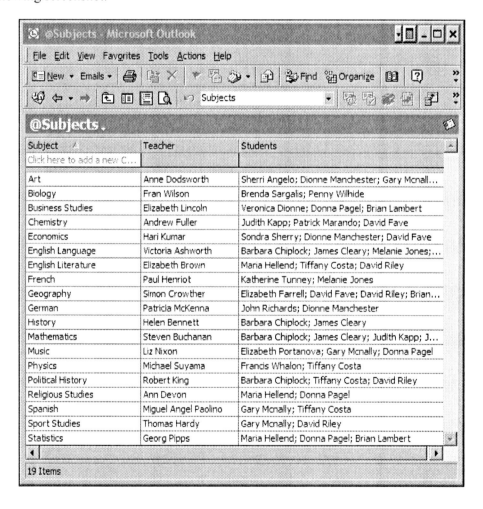

Creating the Teachers Contacts Folder

1. Create a new Contacts folder named @Teachers.

2. Create a new table-type view from the Define Views | New option and name the view Teaching Staff.

3. In the View Summary dialog box, click Fields and select the fields: Full Name, Job Title, Home Address, Home Phone, Mobile Phone, and click OK.

4. We will now create the following new manual fields:

Name	Type	Format	Purpose
Grade	Text	Text	To enter the salary grade of the individual teacher
Weekly Hrs	Number	All digits	To enter the decimal figure that represents the contracted weekly hours

5. And two new formula fields:

Name	In the Formula Field window
Basic Salary	Format(IIf([Grade]="G1","25000",IIf([Grade]="G2","26000",IIf([Grade]="G3","28000",IIf([Grade]="G4","30000","no grade")))),"currency")
Actual Ann Salary	Format([Basic Salary]*[Weekly Hrs],"currency")

6. Exit the View Summary and from the Format Columns dialog box rename the following field as shown:

Field name	New name
Job Title	Subject

What Just Happened?

We have created a folder in which to record the details of the teaching staff of Our School. We have the basic data of address and telephone numbers and we have also included a salary calculation based upon the salary grade of the individual. The salary grade is entered manually into the Grade field and the Basic Salary field will return the correct basic annual salary depending on whether the grade is G1, G2, G3, or G4. Some of the teaching staff do not work full time and their contracted hours expressed as a decimal of weekly hours are entered into the Weekly Hrs field. The field Actual Ann Salary multiplies Basic Salary by Weekly Hrs to produce an actual annual salary as shown in the following section.

The Result

The following screenshot shows Teaching Staff view:

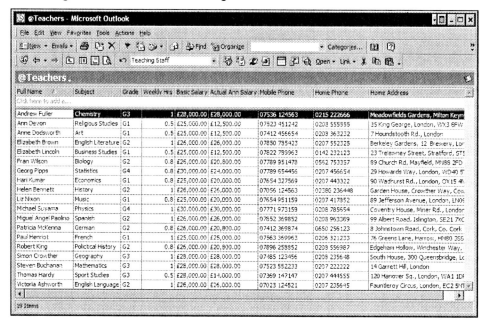

At this point, the teachers' contact records are not linked to any other folder, but once we have created the classes' calendar, we shall link the teachers to their classes. However, there is one more Contacts folder to create and that is for the classrooms.

Creating the Classrooms Contacts Folder

1. Create a new Contacts folder named @Classrooms.

2. Create a new table-type view from the Define Views | New option and name the view Classrooms.

3. In the View Summary dialog box, click Fields and select the field Full Name and click OK.

4. We will now create the following new manual fields:

Name	Type	Format	Purpose
Capacity	Text	Text	To enter the number of students the room can accommodate
Notes	Text	Text	To enter comments about the rooms

Outlook will not allow you to create a new field that has the same name as a standard Outlook field such as, in this case, Notes. However, if when you name the field you add a space after the last letter of the name, you can get away with it. We are creating another Notes field because if we use Outlook's standard Notes field, we would have to open the Contacts records to enter data into the field. Data can be entered into a custom Notes field from within the view.

5. Exit the View Summary and from the Format Columns dialog box rename the following field as shown:

Field name	New name
Full Name	Room

What Just Happened?

We have created a folder that contains the details of the Classrooms and other facilities in Our School.

As with our earlier meeting rooms example, we could add an extra dimension by linking our Classrooms to maintenance tasks, but for this current purpose we shall be linking these rooms only to the classes in a calendar to ensure that the rooms are fully utilized and not double-booked. It is also useful to include sports areas in order to manage sports facilities and to monitor when they are available.

The Result

The following screenshot shows Classrooms view:

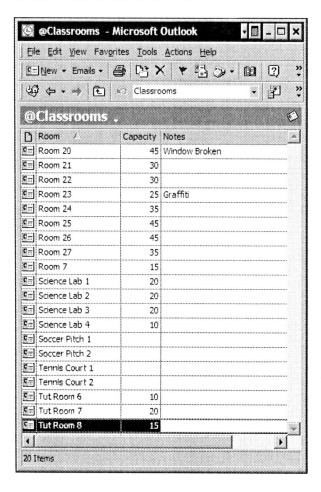

Assigning the Classes Calendar Folders

In Our School, each subject has its own calendar and each day there are sessions in that subject. A typical day in the History calendar at Our School would have Registration, the History classes, Breaks and Lunch shown as appointments and the calendar would operate in the basic Day/Week/Month type view as shown in the screenshot opposite.

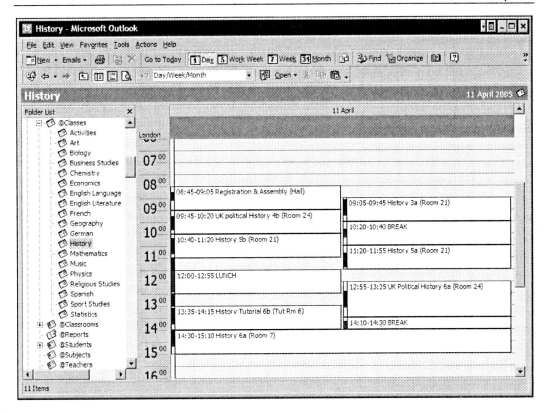

The appointments (classes) in each calendar are assigned to the appropriate subject category so that all classes in the History calendar are assigned to the History category. They are also linked to the rooms in which they will take place and to the subject teacher. So the Activities tab of Room 21, for example, will show all the classes taking place in that room and in the following screenshot we can match the classes in the History calendar taking place in Room 21 with the items shown on the Activities tab of Room 21:

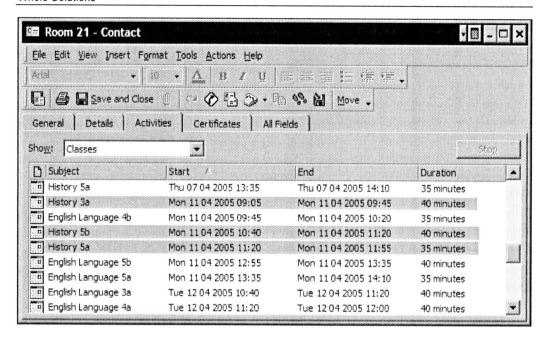

Likewise, the Activities tab of the contacts record of the History teacher, Helen Bennett will show all the classes that she has.

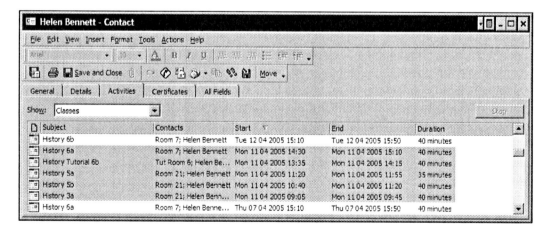

When the class teacher records which students have attended the class, the information can also be recorded in Outlook by linking the students' contacts records with the relevant classes in the appropriate calendar.

For example, student Barbara Chiplock's subjects are English Language, History, and Mathematics and we can verify that from her Contacts record:

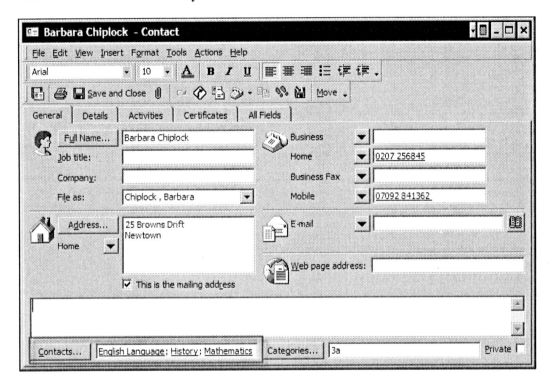

The classes that Barbara attends are linked to her Contacts record and will show on her Activities tab. The items will have already been assigned to the subject categories in the calendar and the Activities tab can be set to group items by category. The following is the result and we can see that Barbara did attend the History class on 11th April:

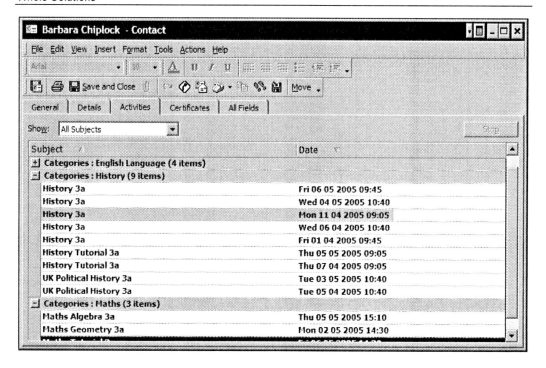

Creating the Assignments Tasks Folder

Because we wish to monitor the progress of the Tasks that we assign to the students and receive updates from them on their progress, this Tasks folder needs to be the default Tasks folder and we will create the following view:

1. Create a new table-type view from the Define Views | New option and name the view Student Assignments.

2. In the View Summary dialog box, click Fields and select the fields: Complete, Subject, Status, Due Date, Contacts, and click OK.

3. We will now create the following new manual fields:

Name	Type	Format	Purpose
Mark	Text	Text	To enter the mark given to the assignments
Full Marks	Number	All digits	To enter the full mark for the assignment
Pass Mark	Number	All digits	To enter the pass mark for the assignment

4. And add the following three new formula fields:

Name	In the Formula Field window
Days Overdue	IIf([Complete]=True,"",IIf(Date()-[Due Date]<0,"",Format(Date()-[Due Date]) & " days"))
Pass/Fail	IIf([Mark]>=[Pass Mark],"Pass","Fail")
% Mark	Format([Mark]/[Full Marks],"percent")

5. Set Group By to Categories, Then by to Contacts (not to be shown in the view), and Then by to Status.

6. Set Sort items by to Due Date.

7. From the Automatic Formatting option, amend the first rule then click Add to create the second of the following formatting rules:

Formatting Rule	Font Format
Completed and Read tasks	Gray Font only (deselect strikeout)

Formatting Rule Name	Field	Condition	Value	Font Format
Not Started	Status	Equals	Not Started	Red

8. Exit the View Summary and from the Format Columns dialog box rename the following field as shown:

Field name	New name
Contacts	Student

What Just Happened?

We have created a view of the default Tasks folder from which Tasks can be assigned to students with a due date and which assignments will be graded and the grade recorded against the Tasks.

To begin with the Days Overdue field will tell us by how many days the due date has been exceeded and the first part of the formula ensures that it will not calculate where tasks have been completed. The remainder of the formula calculates and returns the difference between the current date and the Due Date.

The Pass/Fail field compares the value in the Mark field with the value in the Pass Mark field and returns Pass or Fail appropriately.

The % Mark field calculates the percentage of the Full Marks that the assignment has received. Error messages in this field are the result of there being no value in the Mark field.

The Tasks are grouped first by Category, which is the class name, secondly by the student (the renamed Contacts field), and thirdly by the task status.

The Tutor may wish to be alerted to those assignments that students have not yet started and these are formatted in Red font.

The Result

Here is the Students Assignments view of the Tasks folder:

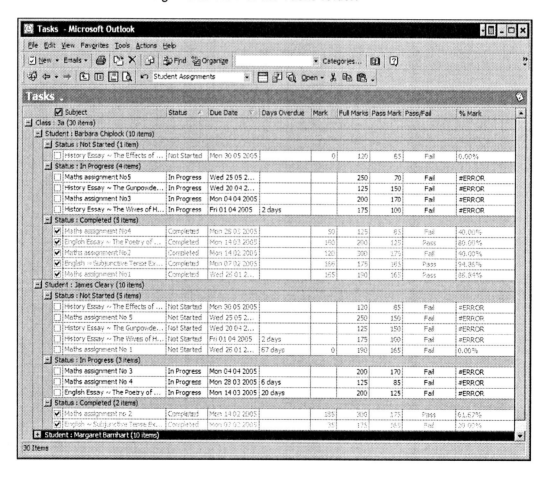

Tasks, having been assigned by a subject teacher, will appear in their Tasks folder awaiting updates from students; also if the teacher maintains student records in a Contacts folder in their Outlook installation, the assignments will also appear on the Activities tab of the student Contacts record.

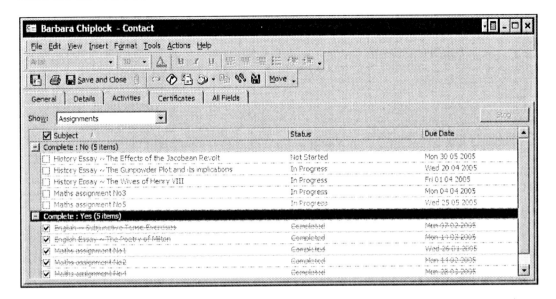

Creating the Journal Reports Folder

We are now going to create a Journal folder that will contain links to the students' progress reports.

1. Create a new Journal folder named @Reports

2. Create a new table-type view from the Define Views | New option and name the view Student Reports.

3. In the View Summary dialog box, click Fields and select the fields: Icon, Attachment, Entry Type, Subject, Size, and Contacts, and click OK.

4. Set Group By to Categories and Then by to Contacts.

5. Exit the View Summary and from the Format Columns dialog box rename the following field as shown:

Field name	New name
Contacts	Student

6. Return to the View Summary dialog box, click Group by, and deselect Show field in View relating to Group by Contacts, to remove the Contacts field from the field header bar, and click OK.

What Just Happened?

We have created a Journal folder named @Reports that contains links to student progress reports that are held elsewhere on the system network.

To store a link in this folder to a student's report, create a new Journal entry and assign it to the category that is the relevant class category of the student (e.g. 3a). Click the Contacts button, locate the student contact record to link the Journal entry to the student and from the Insert | File menu, locate the report in your computer system and insert a shortcut to the student's report.

The Result

Here is the Student Reports view of the Journal folder:

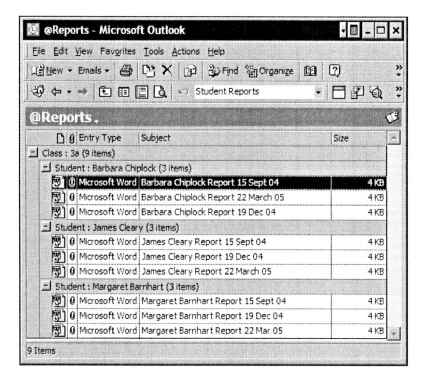

The progress reports can now be opened by clicking the item in the Journal folder or the link that will appear on the Activities tab of the student Contacts record.

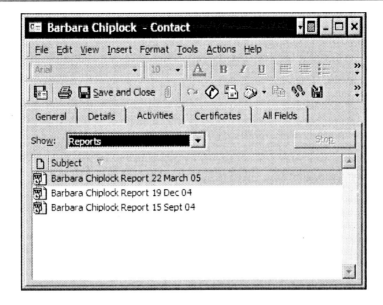

Creating the Notes Folder

The final link in this solution, Our School is the Notes folder, and in Our School, Notes is used to record detentions. Fortunately, the students are pretty well behaved:

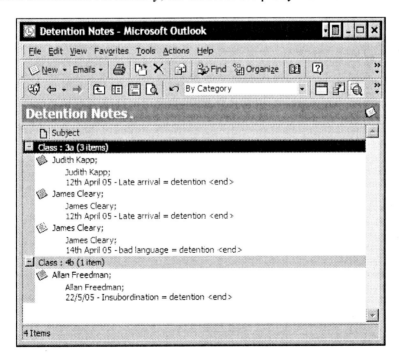

The Notes folder has been set up with just the one field, Subject, and the view that is applied is the predefined By Category view with AutoPreview. The Notes are assigned the category of the class of the student concerned and are colored pink or blue according to the gender of the offender. The Notes are linked to the student's contact record, completing the record of the student's career at Our School.

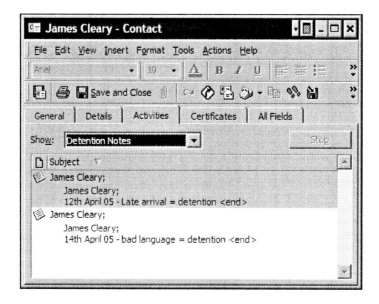

Summary

This book has gradually revealed the untapped power of Outlook's individual components, and in this final chapter, we have brought these components together to create effective procedures for managing information without third-party programs or programmers.

These final interactive solutions emphasize the importance of acknowledging Outlook as a whole application and utilizing the interdependence of its parts.

These complete solutions also demonstrate Outlook's outstanding capabilities as an unmitigated information manager.

Index

E

expenses calendar
about, 32
calendar view, 33
formula fields, 33
manual fields, 33

F

Filter tab, 7
folder views, tasks, 59
folders, Outlook
Calendar, 5
Contacts, 41
Tasks, 57
Format Columns dialog box, 11, 20
formula fields, 11, 18

G

goods/services suppliers view
contacts view, 43
manual fields, 44
Group By option, 30, 33

H

Header/Footer tab, 8

I

induction checklist, reusable tasks, 85
invoicing meeting room bookings, meeting room management, 96

J

journal reports folder, school solution, 129

L

leave calendar, 15
Length of Service view, Contacts folder, 47
linking folders, 15
linking tasks to contacts, 67

M

maintenance, meeting room management, 102
Master Category List button, 6
meeting room calendar view, meeting room management, 91
meeting room management
about, 87
appointment form, 97
calendar view, bookings, 106
invoicing bookings, 96
maintenance, 102
meeting room calendar view, 91
meeting rooms view, 90
orders mail folder, 109
meeting rooms calendar, 88
meeting rooms view, meeting room management, 90
meetings checklist, reusable tasks, 83
meetings schedule
about, 5
calendar view, 6
result, 8
Microsoft Outlook folders. *See* **folders, Outlook**
My expenses view, expenses calendar, 32
My Tasks view
creating the view, 64
filters, 65

N

New Field tab, 11
notes folder, school solution, 131

O

orders mail folder, meeting room management, 109
Outlook Calendar folder, 5
Outlook folders. *See* **folders, Outlook**
Outlook tasks. See **tasks**

P

priority settings, tasks, 58

Printed in the United Kingdom
by Lightning Source UK Ltd.
109378UKS00002BA/3-10